How to Do it!

No matter what it is, the important question always is, "How to do it?"

The mind has many marvelous powers—far more than you have ever dreamed of—and humanity has barely begun the wonderful evolutionary journey that will let us tap into them all at will. We grow in our abilities as we do things.

There are many wonderful things you can do. As you do them, you learn more about the innate qualities of mind and spirit, and as you exercise these inner abilities, they will grow in strength—as will your vision of your mental and spiritual potential.

In learning to do Automatic Writing, or making a Love Charm or using a Magic Mirror, or many other strange and wonderful things, you are extending—just a little bit—the tremendous gift that lies within, the Life Force itself.

We are born that we may grow, and not to use this gift—not to grow in your perception and understanding of it—is to turn away from the gifts of Life, of Love, of Beauty, of Happiness that are the very reason for Creation.

Learning how to do these things is to open psychic windows to New Worlds of Mind & Spirit. Actually doing these things is to enter New Worlds. Each of these things that we do is a step forward in accepting responsibility for the worlds that you can shape and influence.

Simple, easy to follow, yet so very rewarding. Following these step-by-step instructions can start you upon high adventure. Gain control over the world around you, and step into New Worlds of Mind and Spirit.

About the Author

Edain McCoy was born in South Bend, Indiana, to parents of diverse ethnic and religious backgrounds who always encouraged her to explore the history of religious thought. As a teenager she began seeking the roots of her birth religion. That search, and her increasing feminist outlook, eventually brought her back to the Old Religion. A graduate of the University of Texas, Edain now lives in the Midwest where she is continuing her formal graduate studies in cultural history. She is active with the local Irish Arts Association.

To Write the Author

If you wish to contact the author or would like more information about this book, please write to her in care of Llewellyn Worldwide, and we will forward your request. Both the author and publisher appreciate hearing from you and learning of your enjoyment of this book and how it has helped you. Llewellyn Worldwide cannot guarantee that every letter written to the author can be answered, but all will be forwarded. Please write to:

Edain McCoy
℅ Llewellyn Worldwide
P.O. Box 64383-K662, St. Paul, MN 55164-0383, U.S.A.
Please enclose a self-addressed, stamped envelope for reply, or $1.00 to cover costs. If outside the U.S.A. enclose international postal reply coupon.

Free catalog

For more than 90 years Llewellyn has brought its readers knowledge in the fields of metaphysics and human potential. Learn about the newest books in spiritual guidance, natural healing, astrology, occult philosophy and more. Enjoy book reviews, new age articles, a calendar of events, plus current advertised products and services. To get your free copy of *Llewellyn's New Worlds of Mind and Spirit*, send your name and address to:

Llewellyn's New Worlds of Mind and Spirit
P.O. Box 64383-K662, St. Paul, MN 55164-0383, U.S.A.

Llewellyn's "How-To" Vanguard Series

How to Do Automatic Writing

❧ Edain McCoy ❧

1994
Llewellyn Publications
St. Paul, MN 55164-0383, U.S.A.

FIRST EDITION
First Printing, 1994

Cover photograph: Russell Lane
Editing, design and layout: Pamela Henkel

Library of Congress Cataloging-in-Publication Data
McCoy, Edain, 1957—
  How to do automatic writing / Edain McCoy.
  p. cm.
  Includes bibliographical references.
  ISBN 1-56718-662-9
  1. Automatism. 2. Title. 3. Series.
BF 1343.M34 1994
133.9'3--dc20
             94-35157
             CIP

Llewellyn Publications
A Division of Llewellyn Worldwide, Ltd.
P.O. Box 64383, St. Paul, MN 55164-0383

Acknowledgments

The old writer's adage that no one ever authors a book alone was never more true than in the case of this small volume. It could not have come into being without the help of numerous individuals, some of whom may have little or no idea of what a profound influence they were on the final product. Among those to whom I owe a debt of thanks for all their help are: Avigail, my dearest friend from many lifetimes with whom I first brainstormed my ideas; Vanessa, Lianna, and David who were my first Automatic Writing students; "Evelyn from California," whose Automatic Writing first shocked me out of my smug complacency; the wonderful teacher and author, Dick Sutphen, in whose marvelous seminars I first discovered Automatic Writing; my parents, Don and Billie Taylor, who, though they don't always understand what it is I am trying to do, nonetheless remain supportive; and, finally, my husband, Mark, the long-suffering guinea pig for many of my psychic/magickal experiments, who is my cheering section, critic, proofreader, and computer troubleshooter.

And my sincerest appreciation and thanks go, as always, to Nancy Mostad of Llewellyn for her gentle encouragement, and to Trish Telesco, for stirring my creative juices and showing me new ways to expand this simple concept into a worthwhile book.

Contents

❦ 1 ❦

An Introduction to Automatic Writing

My first personal experience with Automatic Writing came in July of 1987 when my husband and I went to the beautiful and mystical red rock canyons of northern Arizona to participate in a seminar on psychicism. These canyons have long been held sacred by the Native Americans who believe them to be inhabited by deities and helpful spirits who often act as catalysts for psychic experiences. Over the past twenty years or so, many others have discovered the powerful spiritual vibrations of these breathtaking canyons which seem to enhance any spell, ritual, divinatory, or other psychic work.

I was greatly impressed by the sheer beauty of the area, and with the undeniable power I felt emanating from the red-hued canyons and cliff walls around me. Even though the sad signs of commercialization were marring many of the spectacular views and, in some cases, cutting off public access to sacred sites, the magnetism of the place was still a powerful draw for anyone with even a modicum of interest in or talent for spiritual and psychic growth.

What I was not impressed with, however, was the Automatic Writing exercise we were asked to do while at the seminar. By this time in life I had learned that virtually anyone could open the channels to their innate psychic abilities, but I strongly doubted that Automatic Writing was an ability worth developing. The whole process seemed to me a frivolous waste of time.

The man conducting the exercise was, and still is, a well-respected leader in the New Age movement, whose work and teachings I have always admired. But the thought of sitting around in a tranced-out blue funk, holding a pen and paper while waiting for some divine inspiration to come through them of their own accord, struck me as ridiculous.

I had not gone to the seminar as much for the content of it as to allow myself time in the sacred space to commune with nature and my deities and to enhance my own spellwork. At the time I was seeking answers as to why I had suffered two miscarriages and was then having trouble conceiving again. In the way of many women faced with fertility problems, I had became obsessed with baby madness, and the most frustrating part of it all was that no doctor could pinpoint a reason for my difficulty.

While in Arizona I did Tarot spells, rock spells, and herbal spells. I had geode stones on my dresser, a Tarot spread laid out in my suitcase, wheat stalks surrounding the bed, special essential oil blends for my bath, and little drawings of babies all tied up in a little totem bag which I wore around my waist like a twisted umbilical cord. While there, I regressed myself to see if my troubles lay in a past-life, and I even ended up learning how to gain some control over my astral projections. But despite all these glorious efforts, the answers to my fertility problems still eluded me.

The afternoon I was to first experience Automatic Writing was hot, sunny, and dry, the sort of southwestern summer day that drains all powers of concentration and will power from those unaccustomed to the climate. I was irritable and dog-tired from the long days of constant psychic experiments, even though they had all been amazingly successful.

Our leader spent a good deal of time explaining to us what Automatic Writing was, and he presented us with his own technique for doing it. I listened to everything he said with the sieve-like ears of a born skeptic. As much as I admired the man, I wasn't convinced.

Then he asked us each to look around the room and team up with a stranger in order to give the process a fair try. I, along with many others, including my husband, was not enthused. I had to force a smile on my face as I teamed up with the nearest unattached stranger. We exchanged brief hellos and avoided further conversation that might color the Automatic Writing we were about to try. All we knew was that she was Evelyn from California and I was Edain from Texas.

With the amenities out of the way, we left the seminar room and sought a quiet place in the bright sunshine near the hotel pool where we could work together. There we sat, face to face, on two sterile vinyl-covered deck chairs, our notepads balanced on our knees, while we each in our own way took ourselves into a meditative state of mind, making an attempt to contact each others' Spirit Guides (another concept I was not sure I fully accepted at the time), in order to provide our partner with some earth-shattering tidbit of personal information.

When I opened my eyes to write I was profoundly bothered by the fact that absolutely no flashes of inspiration and insight were forthcoming. To make matters worse, out of the corner of my eye I could see that Evelyn was writing fast and furious, her pen gliding easily over the glistening white page, while I sat making scribbles in an effort to come up with something—anything—that might actually pass for being divinely inspired. The more I tried the worse it became.

I realized quickly that my own skepticism was partly responsible for blocking my energy flow, as well as the fact that I had always associated this practice with the controversial Ouija™ board. The truth was that I was afraid to let just any old thing come through me. So I mentally cast a protective circle around myself just as I had been doing for rituals in my earth religion for many years. I decided I would not allow anything negative to work through me, and I evoked the power of my Goddess for guidance and aid.

After I had done these things I began to relax, and with relaxation I began to get random impressions that I couldn't ignore. Though I was far from writing madly, my pen being driven by some unseen force and spelling out words in a hand unfamiliar to me, I did feel I had latched onto something which might be worth writing down. I was profoundly disturbed when I found that I was writing about Evelyn's need to connect with other people who shared her interests, that she was allowing herself to be lonely and isolated when she didn't have to be. I was also writing down tips on how she and her husband could improve their flagging marital relationship.

When we were both finished and fully back in our everyday consciousness, Evelyn asked me to go first. I looked uneasily at the pathetic few notes I had jotted down, and wondered if I had any right to say such personal things to a woman I didn't know a thing about. But there I sat with notes in hand, and I knew I had to say something. I decided to go for broke, hoping I could somehow blame any outright rudeness on some hapless Spirit Guide. I apologized in advance, and then read her my brief page.

I'm not sure who was more surprised, her when she heard what I'd written, or me when she was able to understand and identify with everything on the page. She told me she was indeed lonely, and that she had come to the seminar with some women she didn't really know very well while her husband went to the Mediterranean for a few weeks. She felt she was searching for answers to questions that she had been unable to identify until I'd read her my notes.

I was pleased that Evelyn was happy with the words I had come up with, and thankful that she was not offended in any way, but I was still far from convinced that I had been the vessel for a message from Evelyn's Spirit Guide, or any other part of her subconscious for that matter. While I have never been gifted as a psychic I have always been highly empathic, and I was wondering if I might not have picked up on an emotional projection of sadness from her and had unconsciously paired that with the fact that she wore a wedding ring but was obviously not at the seminar with her mate. Simple logic. An old sooth-sayer's parlor trick. I remained a skeptic and I was still waiting to be convinced about the merits of Automatic Writing.

I must confess, in retrospect, that I was not altogether unmoved. I suppose I was feeling just a tiny bit smug at my meager success, but still completely doubtful that this woman could contact my own Spirit Guide, if indeed such a creature existed, least of all tell me anything of any value that I could not discover for myself.

I sat back in the sticky vinyl deck chair expecting to hear the usual banal platitudes uttered by amateur channelers world over. I was waiting to be told something poetic and full of sloppy sentiment such as, "Tend the garden of your heart and watch your love grow," or some other cliche. I believed anyone could write words generic enough in nature that they could be applied to anyone's life.

As had I, Evelyn also apologized for what she was about to read to me. She said it made no sense to her, but she'd say it anyway since the information came from my Guide whose name was Sandra. I forced myself to suppress a complacent smile.

Sandra? How dull. I had really hoped for something more exotic. By now I was convinced that Evelyn had no imagination at all and that her alleged Spirit Guide communication would prove less than entertaining.

Then Evelyn read her Automatic Writing.

You can image how I almost fell out of my seat, and right into that blasted luke-warm swimming pool, when the first words out of her mouth were:

"So, when are you going to ask me about the baby?"

The rest of the words she read to me were lost in a fog. I was dumfounded! There was no way this woman could have known, or even guessed, that I was baby-obsessed at the time of the experiment. In fact, there were no words she could have uttered that would have shaken me more profoundly, or convinced me that there might be something to this Automatic Writing stuff after all.

I was still a little weak-kneed from the experience as Evelyn and I returned to the spacious seminar room where we had been instructed to gather after our little experiment was over. We quickly found my husband, Mark, and Evelyn's friend, with whom he had been partnered. Mark wore the same stupefied expression as me.

"How'd you do?" I asked him quietly, when I was sure no one else could hear us.

"I couldn't do it at all," he admitted. "But would you believe my partner's writing mentioned babies?"

At that point, I was hooked!

I decided I wanted to explore this oracle further, but knew I couldn't work with the technique given me that day, and I found that the few other available methods would not work for me either. To make my search even more frustrating, I discovered that there were no books on the market that covered the subject in any depth. I also tried to find an old friend, the only person I knew personally who claimed to be able to make Automatic Writing work (and how I wish now that I'd paid attention to her when I had the chance). But the search for her, and all my other investigations, came to a dead end.

After several months of this futile search for knowledge, I decided that I would have to develop my own techniques, ones more suited to my psyche and to the needs of those who, like myself, did not find this an oracle easy to use at first. I decided that I had to confirm in my own mind what the process was all about, how to best channel other intelligences, protect myself from harm, keep records of my work, etc.

This book is the result of my findings. The method I teach is easy to use. It is simple and straightforward in practice, and contains enough ritual and imagery that most New Age thinkers can relate to its theories and concepts. My efforts also taught me that anyone can learn to use Automatic Writing and be able to receive guidance and commentary on all imaginable issues. It is not difficult, and most people have some degree of success fairly quickly. This process is not like a complex ritual that requires a special collection of fancy tools and memorized speeches. Unlike spellwork it does not require intense and clear visualization. And, unlike prayer, it does not rely on any outside being for success. It does not even ask that you give your allegiance to any one deity, or to surrender to a particular religious philosophy. All it takes is a sound understanding of the whats and hows surrounding it, and concentrated practice.

The techniques presented in this slender volume are the ones that work for me and for the people I taught. They represent the maximum effort of the time and energy you will probably have to invest in learning Automatic Writing. Most people pick it up long before they finish all the teachings and preliminary exercises. A few, like myself, will take a little longer.

The key to unlocking this oracle is persistence, practice, and a willingness to keep an open mind.

❧ 2 ❧
What Is
Automatic Writing?

Before engaging in Automatic Writing most individuals have a few questions they want, and need, to have answered. Getting clear, honest answers dispels rumors, and puts people at ease. This chapter addresses those common concerns.

• What is Automatic Writing?

Automatic Writing is the art of contacting other intelligences through the use of a pen (or pencil) and paper while in an altered, or meditative, state of consciousness. People wishing to perform this art hold a writing tool over a blank piece of paper, slow and clear their minds, and allow themselves to be a channel for communications from other entities or from their own Higher Self.

The writing is called "automatic" because that's how it feels. You plug into the energy of the entity with whom you are communicating and they do the writing, often leaving you unaware of what is being written until it is over. Once you gain control of the process your hand moves as if it has a life of its own, without your volition, and will often tingle as if it has indeed briefly been a part of someone else.

Unfortunately, most people's conceptions of Automatic Writing come from poorly produced horror films of the 1930s and 1940s that grossly distorted and exaggerated the process. In truth, Automatic Writing is not all that dramatic.

This oracle is similar to the trance-channeling that gained popularity among New Age thinkers several years ago. The difference being that, with Automatic Writing, there are no big mysteries to uncover, no single entity who becomes your own personal property, and anyone can learn to do it successfully with the investment of only a bit of time and effort.

• Where and when did Automatic Writing begin?

As divinatory oracles go, Automatic Writing is relatively young when compared to ancient systems like the Tarot cards. Part of this is due to the fact that common literacy is also a relatively youthful phenomenon in the annals of human history. Until the late nineteenth century the typical household, even in the technologically advanced West, did not usually keep pens and paper at hand. These were considered a luxury of the well-to-do.

There is sketchy evidence to suggest that Automatic Writing was in use as early as the late sixteenth century in the court of England's Elizabeth I, who was known to have a fascination with the occult. But the poor country folk still relied on dreams, and nature's other symbolic languages, for their divination needs.

In the fifteenth and sixteenth centuries, several other European monarchs reportedly employed psychics and standard court astrologers, but whether or not they used Automatic Writing is uncertain.

Automatic Writing did not become widely popular until the mid-nineteenth century when the Spiritualist movement began to gain momentum. Spiritualists are a small Christian sect who believe that the dead offer advice from beyond the grave to living friends and relatives. This group used the process heavily and, in many cases, inappropriately. Automatic Writing became less reputable as more frauds and con-artists were attracted to the profit potential of this burgeoning market. Unfortunately, the negative attention, including an official Congressional investigation, blurred the lines between authentic communications and the more often produced stage illusions.

In the midst of all the hype and attention that inevitably accompanies any new fad, there is always a core of truth. Most notably, in 1855, a

French magistrate turned psychic investigator, named Alec Rivail, was invited to the home of the Baudin sisters at the request of their father, who claimed his otherwise flighty daughters regularly received profound messages through their use of Automatic Writing. Rivail, known as one of the first professionals in the now well-established field of psychic research, was greatly impressed with the penetrating insights and range of knowledge demonstrated by the otherwise unimpressive young ladies, including some rather concrete answers to several technical questions dealing with the hard sciences of which the ladies had no knowledge.

The Baudin sisters were not the only ones producing hard-to-dismiss Automatic Writing throughout the remainder of the Victorian period, and just enough of it was forthcoming to keep the interest among the general populace of Europe until well into the early twentieth century. The master of logic, Sir Arthur Conan Doyle, author of the Sherlock Holmes mysteries, was a champion of this art. He and his wife often used Automatic Writing to communicate with their son who had been killed in action in World War I.

In the United States, by the turn of the century, the line between fraudulent and sincere mediums was even more obscure than it was in Europe. The American Spiritualist movement had begun back in 1848 when a young American girl named Margaret Fox was exploited as a medium by her fortune-seeking father. The yellow press fell on the story like a vulture on a carcass, and a craze was born. Soon every community and clique had its own professional Automatic Writer who often worked without benefit of writing instrument, but allowed the "spirits" to write "freely" on a sealed blackboard.

In the post World War I years, the famous escape artist and illusionist, Harry Houdini, who was a master in the art of theatrical trickery, attempted to expose the frauds. He sincerely believed that communication with discarnate intelligences was possible, and he was willing to offer a lavish reward to prove it. He pledged to pay $10,000 to any medium on the planet who could provide him with conclusive proof that they had indeed contacted his own mother. Houdini publicly claimed that he never found a single medium whose tricks he was not able to unmask, though later evidence suggests that he perhaps found one or two—including Mrs. Arthur Conan Doyle—whose Automatic Writing he found hard to disregard.

Still, the promise of money and fame to be found in mediumship continued to be an attractive lure for scoundrels, and, eventually, the United States Congress was asked to investigate and, if necessary, regulate the fortunetelling industry under which the question of Spiritualism, and of Automatic Writing, fell at that time. The issue was one of the most volatile of the 1920s; serious constitutional issues were at stake, such as the right of free enterprise, free speech, and freedom of religion.

By this time the damage was done. The Spiritualist movement, with its attendant interest in Automatic Writing, hit its peak in the 1920s, after which only the truly dedicated remained within the faith. People were fed up with the side show. With the coming of the Great Depression in 1929, the pastime of Automatic Writing faded into oblivion as more serious matters—such as how to feed a family—took the time and attention of people on both sides of the Atlantic.

Today, Automatic Writing is still used in the Spiritualist churches, much as it is by New Agers, Pagans, and High Magicians who have been rediscovering it as a reliable method of divination.

Over the past decade there has been a renewed interest in the process, but its secrets have remained in the hands of popular channelers and avowed psychics who often try to tell the rest of us that when we are as "enlightened" (be cautious of that word) as they are, then the secret of the process will be revealed to us.

Perhaps because it is one of the easiest and most fascinating oracles to use, those who wish to remain in control of it do not like the idea of sharing its power. There are no abstract symbols to interpret, no flowery language (usually) to sift through, and no cultural lore attached to the process. In most cases a simple, straightforward answer communicated in one's own language is the result. Some secret, huh?

• How can I use Automatic Writing?

Automatic Writing can be used like any other oracle. You can receive commentaries, ideas, guidance, advice, and information from your own Higher Self, or from any other entity you wish to try and contact. You can learn about your past-lives, uncover forgotten memories of childhood, retrieve lost objects, communicate with deceased family and friends, or divine future potentials.

The entire Automatic Writing process will be fully outlined in Chapters Five and Six, and they will provide you with more ideas on how the oracle can work for you, whom you can contact, and what you can learn from them.

Sometimes people get so fascinated by a divination process that they end up using it solely for personal entertainment. While this is not inherently wrong, repeated use of Automatic Writing with no greater purpose in mind can result in it becoming every bit as useless to you as a video game. It will remain an entertainment, a party trick to "amaze and delight" your friends. Its beneficial powers will diminish, and you could even end up attracting negative entities to your writing. On a larger scale, you could even damage Automatic Writing's reputation as a valid oracle, as was done in the 1920s.

One question frequently asked by beginners is if they can do readings (another name for divination) for others. Like other oracles, Automatic Writing works best when it is done for yourself, though you can, when requested, get an accurate reading for other people. But you would be better off to teach them to use the process for themselves if they are serious about using it as a means of divination on a regular basis.

You should never read for others without their knowledge and consent as this is a form of spying and manipulation. Because I am a Pagan, I always cite the Threefold Law to people I teach who are tempted to venture out on this destructive path. The law states that any energy you send forth, whether good or bad, will be revisited on you three times over. But don't take my word for it. Look into the teaching of any religion or system of ethics and you will find that eventual retribution for willful wrongs is a universal theme.

And if those warnings aren't enough for you, consider the other risks. You are somewhat vulnerable when you open yourself as a channel, even with your protective rituals and icons in place. Do you really want to risk harming yourself by practicing a negative art, and possibly draw into yourself the lower entities and energies that might be attracted to your misuse of the oracle?

• How does Automatic Writing work?

While no one can say for sure exactly what it is that makes an oracle work, there is one accepted theory around which all other possible answers base themselves.

Automatic Writing is a tool of divination. Through merging ourselves with a universal mental energy, usually referred to as the Collective Unconscious, our Higher Self (sometimes called the super-conscious) can access information in this great mass of omniscient energy and relay it to us. As we live each minute exercising our free will, we change and shape the information recorded in the Collective Unconscious so that— to use a term from modern physics—a probability matrix is formed that increases or decreases as the event in question draws near. It is from these probabilities that we get our answers.

When not divining the future, this mass of collective power can still be tapped to generate the energy needed to contact other entities.

Another theory for how such contacts operate is put forth by renowned psychic researchers Brad and Sherry Steiger in their book *Undying Love*, a work which explores documented contact with human discarnates. Pointing out that we human beings use only about 1 percent of our brains' total capacity over the course of an entire lifetime, the authors hypothesize that perhaps in that vast unused 99 percent there are messages being received and exchanged with the etheric realms all the time, and that a few gifted persons ("mediums" if you like the term) are able to tap into those exchanges from time to time.

It is my belief that the rest of us can teach ourselves to successfully tap into those channels of communication with meditation and practice. Hopefully, as humanity grows and matures, and if we can prevent ourselves from destroying the planet and each other in the meantime, we will evolve into using those uncharted regions of the brain to reach goals and gain knowledge that today are only the stuff of storybooks. After all, those things that were mere fantasy to our ancestors have become reality for us. And with advances in theoretical physics, there is little left which is not—at the very least—theoretically possible for us to achieve. Certainly contact and communication with other dimensions would fall into those great achievements.

• Is Automatic Writing safe?

Though a lot of chatter is heard in the New Age community about psychic attack, I personally know of no instances of this happening. True cases of psychic attack are almost unheard of, which is why they tend to make headlines. Even in these extreme cases, about half of them can be logically explained by means that have nothing to do with other-worldly events or inhabitants.

Automatic Writing is just a tiny bit riskier than the so-called "safe" oracles such as the Tarot cards, where your own Higher Mind (sometimes called your Deep Mind) answers your questions. In any process where you seek to contact other intelligences and allow them the use of your body, you run the risk of encountering unpleasant entities. Because of this, many people who use Automatic Writing play it safe and choose to contact only their own Higher Self, knowing it has the ability to contact on their behalf anyone else with whom they may wish to speak.

But don't let fear hold you back. There are many ways to protect yourself from the remote possibility of harm. Chapter Five will give you numerous ideas on how to do this, and at least one of these methods should appeal to and work for you.

In fairness, you should be aware that there have actually been several reported cases where people have opened these Automatic Writing channels only to find themselves taken over, but be assured that such occurrences are extremely rare. If you adequately protect yourself beforehand you should encounter no troubles. If you do, you should repeat your protection rituals daily and not engage in Automatic Writing for at least a month. This last part is simply common sense. If you do not open the channel you cannot be bothered.

You should also avoid Automatic Writing if you receive messages that are threatening, demanding, coercive, crude, or ask you to do things which are against your principles. Again, allow time to distance yourself from the problem (about a month), and then double your protection and try again when you feel comfortable. If your problems persist it would be wise to contact a therapist trained in and sympathetic to New Age ideas.

Despite all the anti-New Age hype from the popular press, be assured that, all things considered, most occult endeavors are safer than crossing a city street.

• Can I get stuck in a trance while doing this?

First of all, stories of people being "stuck" in altered states of consciousness are largely exaggerated, and the few tales that are true are usually from the annals of psychologists and other medical professionals who regularly use deep level hypno-therapy when dealing with mentally and emotionally disturbed patients. The medium-level altered state you will place yourself in for Automatic Writing cannot sever your connection with the outside world. Though you will be intently focused on your efforts, you will not be completely unaware of where you are and what you are doing. In fact, for the actual writing portion of the process, your eyes will be opened, and you will find that you have to force yourself to stay in an altered state rather than forcing yourself out of one.

There is a phenomenon often confused with being "stuck" that is common to any shift in consciousness, and that is known as Time Distortion. When we take ourselves out of everyday waking consciousness, time no longer has meaning. How many times have you awakened from a deep sleep and looked at your alarm clock, expecting it to be nearly time to get up, only to discover that you have only been asleep for a few hours? Or how many times have you hurriedly roused yourself from a nap, fearing you have slept through the entire night, just to find to your relief that only a few minutes have passed? This is Time Distortion.

During Automatic Writing you will usually bring yourself out of your altered state as soon as the communication to you has stopped, which will take at the very most about thirty minutes. However, if you are truly afraid that time will get away from you during this or any other psychic exercise, you can either set a soft alarm for yourself or ask someone to awaken you after a pre-determined time has elapsed.

• Can I cause myself physical harm?

You will not lose control of your body parts, harm your nerves, hand, or any other part of your body by practicing Automatic Writing. You will be channeling psychic energy only—energy that already exists around you every single day. The only difference is that during Automatic Writing you are seeking to temporarily harness it to work for you. It cannot physically hurt you.

• Will I be able to stop the process if needed?

In a word—YES. You will always be in control of the process and of all your faculties while in an altered state of consciousness. If you don't like what is being written or have an emergency to tend to, you will be fully able to deal with those things, often handling them more capably than you would if you had not first been in that fully relaxing, mind-expanding state of consciousness.

Usually the automatic communication will go on for no more than a single page of standard notebook paper and then it will stop, so you will not be tied up with it for a long period of time. If you are able to perceive what is being written to you as it happens, and you decide you don't like it, simply let go of your pen and stop. Remember, it's your hand.

• What does Automatic Writing feel like?

Different people feel the Automatic Writing process in different ways, though there are some sensations common to the experience.

First of all, you are not in a deep trance from which you cannot emerge if you wish to do so, and, as previously mentioned, you will always be in control. You will be in a medium-level altered state of consciousness in which you will be focused on your goal, but not completely unaware of the world around you. You will probably feel as you do when you are in a light sleep or are daydreaming.

Your hand may or may not feel as if it has been momentarily "taken over," but if it is, and you find this is a feeling that you do not enjoy, you can simply stop what you are doing.

Your hand may tingle a bit, as might your writing arm or the top of your head, or it might feel as if it is very heavy or very light.

You may also see gentle lights around you. This is common to altered state experiences and is often thought of as a place known as the astral plane coming into your field of vision. Usually these lights are white, misty, and vaporous, rather like a low flying cloud, but they can be colored. Flame colors and blues are the hues most often seen at this time. As long as they do not appear dark and ugly, they are nothing to fear.

Another common experience is the sensation of having great personal power flowing from deep within you. This is not only natural, but a good sign that you are drawing upon the vast resources of your innate psychic powers.

You may also experience a feeling of being distanced from yourself, as if you are floating just outside yourself and are watching the Automatic Writing process from a foot or two away from your body. Again, this is a common phenomenon in any psychic work and should not disturb you.

• What sort of questions or issues can Automatic Writing help me with?

Because Automatic Writing deals with the written word it can be very specific and, therefore, can easily target an exact issue or concern you may have. Unlike Tarot or other forms of divination that use picture symbols to communicate, this oracle uses plain, everyday language.

You can ask for an answer to a specific question such as, "Where is my lost wallet?" or something as vague as "What is the possibility that I will change jobs within the next year?" Ask your questions carefully because you will receive answers, even though they may not be the ones you want to hear.

Sometimes you will even receive answers to questions you were only thinking of asking. This phenomenon is well documented among other divinatory processes, commonly called "Psychic Override," and is your Higher Self's way of communicating an important message to you that it might not otherwise have the chance to do. When this happens you will know it.

- Can I get practical help in other occult practices?

By contacting any number of entities through Automatic Writing you can get practical tips on such diverse practices as the best herb to use in a love spell, a new and helpful astral projection technique, ideas for a new ritual you are writing, the name of the best stone to wear to help ease the pain of arthritis, or the possible outcome of any spell or creative visualization you wish you do.

As in any relationship, you should wait until you are comfortable in it, and have built a solid relationship with the entity(s) you regularly contact, before taking too much advice from them. It's simply a matter of building trust.

• How will I know that the answers I receive are true?

Questions dealing with the elusive "truth" of any matter are hard to answer. In order to do so, one almost must solve the age-old question of what reality is. If we choose, for the purposes of this question to define "true" as being something accurate rather than substantive, we may have a better chance of dealing with the heart of the issue rather than its many nuances.

In essence, you won't always know if your writing is "true" as in "accurate," and you should always keep this possibility in mind when working with it.

Again, let's compare Automatic Writing to the Tarot cards. With a Tarot deck your subconscious manipulates the cards to comment upon, or clarify, an issue. Your mind knows all your problems and concerns, and is able to sort them out for you. While you will still have to interpret the symbols of the cards and make informed decisions from them, you can be assured of a clear and truthful picture of the issue. In Automatic

Writing the information you receive will often come from intelligences other than your own. And just because someone is dead, or in spirit, does not make them any smarter, more compassionate or knowledgeable than they were in life. Even the most well-meaning entity may inadvertently steer you in the wrong direction or give you inaccurate information. Use your own powers of reasoning when assessing the value of your Automatic Writing, and never blindly follow any commands but those of your own heart.

Occasionally the manner in which your handwriting comes out will indicate the origin of the information, if that is a concern for you. For example, if you are consulting your dead mother, and the handwriting is unmistakably hers, then chances are you have truly contacted her energy. Whether her advice is sound is another matter. Unfortunately, only a very small percentage of people using Automatic Writing ever find that the handwriting differs from their own. I am one of the many who are still waiting to see that phenomenon happen.

If we choose to define "true" as being something which has truth as the core of the issue, as substance rather than facts, we are again forced to analyze what we see on paper. For example, regard skeptically any writing which shows an inclination to partisanship or bigotry or any other earthly failing that comes through no matter how vague it may be. This may either indicate that your source is not as omniscient and high-minded as you would wish, or it may be your own negative feelings and prejudices are clouding your answers. For example, if you get a writing which implies that certain governments or philosophies are inherently evil, or that certain people are somewhat inferior by virtue of their appearance, then this is definitely not a higher entity speaking. In such cases it is best to shut down the channel for a while until you can determine from where the negative information came.

For instance, I once read an Automatic Writing by someone who used it only to justify his own skewed thinking. The one page he allowed me to see—apparently it was one of his more mild ones—was a diatribe against communism. It is doubtful that discarnate entities really care all that much about human economic systems, and since no such system is inherently good or evil until practiced by fallible and greedy people, there is no such thing as a single, ultimate evil such as this writing was trying to indicate. I tried to gently explain to him that I thought his stream of consciousness was either blocked off from the true sources of expanded knowledge, or else that he was merely manifesting a deep need to justify his own opinions. But the man would not be convinced, and I always feared for his mental balance and safety as he pursued his dangerous communications.

The best way to judge your Automatic Writing is by assessing its value to you over time. This is why keeping records is so important and it will be discussed at length later in the book.

• What about psycho-dramas in Automatic Writing?

Psycho-dramas are vivid fantasies that seem like very real experiences to the ones who have them. They are a part of our dream world, our astral projections, our past-life recalls, even everyday conscious memory can affect Automatic Writing. Sometimes your mind will communicate to you with vivid psycho-dramas to make a point it might otherwise be unable to make.

With this oracle, as with every other aspect of your life, you must rationally examine and analyze your writing to determine if the messages you have received are worthy of your further consideration. This can be done by asking yourself two basic questions: 1) Is this part of my reality? and 2) Is this helpful to me now?

The first question is by far the most difficult of the two to decide. Anyone who has ever experienced past-life regression, or has kept a dream diary, knows how difficult this can be to accomplish. First of all you are a complete entity, your mental, physical, and spiritual bodies are here and now joined in the particular configuration which you call "yourself." You cannot isolate one completely from the other and one area will often blend into another in the depths of your mind which has the ability to store over ten trillion bits of information and memory, most of it locked away in the hard-to-access areas of your subconscious. These memories are a part of you and all have something to contribute to your growth and enjoyment of your current life. If there is some overlap, this is natural, and does not invalidate your efforts. Some people find that what they thought was a great or profound communication was really a memory from a long forgotten incident in childhood, so they dismiss the writing it came from. But it should not matter so much where the information came from. The point is you remembered an otherwise lost piece of valuable knowledge, and presumably you did so at a time when you most needed the help or comfort that information supplied.

The second question is easier to answer and may be all you truly need to think about. If the information or advice you receive in Automatic Writing is helpful, comforting, insightful, and of use to you, then that is what should be important, not whether the event described is "real."

- Can I engage in dialogue while doing Automatic Writing?

At first your communications will be one-sided. In other words, you will go into a receptive mind frame or altered state of consciousness, receive information, and then read it when you are completely finished. If you want to pursue any issue further you will have to do it at another session. This is especially true when you are first learning the process. You will not want to interrupt the flow of words once you get them going by attempting to look at them critically. Save that for when you are experienced in the art, otherwise you will only hamper your progress.

As you progress with your art, and are able to comprehend what is being written as it is happening, you can ask follow-up questions when the writing flow stops. The being you are in contact with should then respond again. You may continue this as long as you can stay in a receptive state, and as long as the entity working with you wants to continue.

- Will my communications always come in my native language?

Rest assured that 99.9 percent of the time your Automatic Writing will be in your primary language, or one in which you are virtually fluent.

No matter how adept you become at any altered state working, you cannot divorce your mind completely from the body which is its home. Any messages you receive during Automatic Writing must first pass through the part of your brain that controls your powers of writing and your use of language skills, therefore you virtually cannot be written to in any language other than your own. Because of the structure of the brain it is rare when any channeling process, either written or verbal, comes across in another language because the hemisphere of your brain that governs writing and speaking (the left) is separate from the one in which memory is stored (the right). This means that any language memory from a past-life, from those few words of Hebrew or Latin you learned as a child in religious school, or from that one semester of Spanish you took in high school, is not stored in a place easily accessible to you during the channeling process, even though all of it is retained somewhere within your subconscious.

Only on very rare occasions does such an occurrence happen. Women experience a higher incidence than men of this phenomenon (known as xeno-escrite when writing, and xenoglossy when speaking) because they generally have more connecting tissues (corpus callosum) linking the two brain hemispheres.

The Esoteric and Technical Associations of the Human Brain Hemispheres

Left Brain	Right Brain
Right Side of Body	Left Side of Body
Active principle	Passive Principle
Projection	Reception
The Sun	The Moon
Mars	Venus
Masculine	Feminine
God	Goddess
Analytical	Synthetical
Rationality	Emotions
Objective	Subjective
Gold	Silver
White	Black
Light	Dark
Language	Memory
Taking Action	Planning to Act
Linear Thought	Non-linear Thought
Lines	Circles
Logic	Creativity
Reason	Intuition
Hearing	Vision
Yin	Yang
Life	Death
Conscious	Sub- and Super-Conscious
Profane	Sacred
Lust	Love
Progression	Regression
Worldly Thoughts	Introspection
Government	Religion
Law and Order	Anarchy and Chaos
Statistics	Supposition
The Visible	The Hidden
Knowledge	Secrets
Oligarchy	Consensus
War	Peace
Blades	Vessels
Waking	Sleeping
Focusing	Dreaming
Beginnings	Endings
Stagnation	Transition
Using Information	Processing Information
Fire	Water
The Present	Past and Future
Bone	Blood

If you do happen to get a communication in a language you don't understand, simply try again, and ask that you be written to in your own tongue. If your request goes repeatedly unheeded, it may be a sign that an unwelcome entity has managed to sneak through your protective barriers, or that you are manifesting an unresolved past difficulty, and you should avoid Automatic Writing for at least a month to give the problem time to go away. Needless to say, if the enigma persists you should either give up on Automatic Writing altogether or seek professional counseling.

• Are there times when I should avoid Automatic Writing?

Common sense should tell you when your body and mind are not up for the strain of psychic work, just as it tells you when you are too sick to go to your job or to school. Basically you should avoid Automatic Writing when you are angry, sick, rushed, preoccupied, or very tired.

Anger is a negative emotion, and when you are angry you are circulating a lot of intense, potentially destructive energy. To carry this into an exercise where you are opening yourself to other realms of consciousness is unwise. First of all there is a possibility you will contact a negative entity who is attracted to your violent mental state and, secondly, there is the possibility that your writing will only anger you further if your Higher Self or Spirit Guides try to calm you before you are ready.

If you are sick you should avoid psychic exercise just as you would avoid a physical workout. If the body is ill it must have time to heal itself without any added strains, and divination, especially the sort of prolonged concentration needed for Automatic Writing, generates a great deal of added stress, much more so than you may realize. For example, my best friend learned to consciously astral project while we were harried undergraduate seniors, after which she came down with a whopper of a cold. I didn't really believe the two events were related, and I forgot about the incident until about a year later. At that time I also learned to astral project when my defenses were weak, and I promptly came down with a nasty cold of my own. Lesson learned: Save any stress on your mind and body for when you are completely well.

If you are preoccupied or rushed you will probably not be successful in your efforts, and you will only frustrate yourself by persisting. And if you are tired you will be unable to adequately protect yourself or to concentrate on your question.

Astrologically speaking, there are no specific times when Automatic Writing should not be done, but there are times that can make it easier or harder to do. See Chapter Four for details on using astrology to aid you.

The weather may also impact your efforts, and this is why keeping a journal of your writing is important. Looking back will show exactly which weather systems effect you positively and negatively. In either case, there is no one weather event you should absolutely avoid.

Any day of the week is fine for Automatic Writing, as are any holidays. Only your own beliefs and religious affiliation can ban a particular day from your divination calendar.

• Do I have to do all the preliminary training exercises in this book first?

You may use the Automatic Writing techniques in this book by following the step-by-step checklist outlined at the end of Chapter Six. You may, however, skip the other exercises that help you to open your chakras if you wish. Many New Age thinkers are already in tune with these subtle energies, are naturally gifted with psychic talents, and can pick up the Automatic Writing process with just the basic instructions.

The meditation skills and chakra exercises outlined in Chapter Five are useful in opening your psychic channels and providing you with concrete imagery to focus your mind on while doing divination work. They also teach the art of meditation to anyone unfamiliar with it, and they show how to channel energy through the chakra system, and how to cleanse and balance these potent energy centers. Whether you wish to use these exercises for your Automatic Writing or not, they can be valuable additions to your regimen of spiritual, physical, and mental well-being.

When you have read through this entire book and still have trouble making the Automatic Writing process work for you, begin again with Chapter Five and practice the exercises given there. If you still are not successful, Chapter Seven provides a lengthy list of tips that can help you learn Automatic Writing.

• How long does it take to learn this process?

As stated above, some people are able to use Automatic Writing after being instructed only in the basic technique, whereas others will have to use all available mental exercises and engage in intense practice in order to master it.

Make a deal with yourself. Give yourself sixty days to make Automatic Writing work for you. If you follow the process given here, and faithfully practice every day—without fail—for two solid months, virtually everyone will be able to have success. All in all, it is probably one of the easiest divinatory oracles to learn to use, and certainly the most fun.

❧ 3 ❧

Who or What You Can Contact

Who and What you seek to communicate with during Automatic Writing is limited only by your imagination and the willingness of those you seek to contact you. Below we will explore the possibilities for contact and what each of them can, and cannot, do for you.

The Higher Self

Probably the most beneficial and safe contact for Automatic Writing is your own Higher Self. This omniscient part of you is not only in constant communication with your physical mind, but also with the collective unconscious, that vast nebulous mass of energy which contains in itself all the knowledge of the universe. Many people who regularly use Automatic Writing never attempt any other contact because of these reasons. The Higher Self is reliable, rarely wrong, readily available, and always has your welfare at heart.

Occultists from many backgrounds have known and documented the power of the Higher Self which seeks to contact you, usually succeeding through dreams and meditation. Opening a direct line of communication with it, such as through Automatic Writing, will help you in ways you might never imagine. It can easily seek information from other sources outside yourself and report back to you, it can help your subconscious retrieve needed information, and it can advise you from a somewhat distanced perspective while still being intimately a part of you. Your Higher Self has access to all things you ever knew in this life, and in those past and future, and can help you unlock your own karmic secrets.

My first Automatic Writing pursued under the technique given in this book was to my Higher Self. I asked it to simply comment on something I needed to know or be aware of, and it complied beautifully. Below is the first part of the text with appropriate punctuation added. Automatic Writing tends to flow quickly, often jumping from issue to issue and sentence to sentence with little or no breaks. Grammar and punctuation are not things spirit beings seem to regard as important.

My Higher Self speaks to me as if it were a number of beings. I do not know the reason for this, nor am I always able to easily interpret the messages it gives me until several weeks pass.

So you believe in us after all,
after your Garden episode we were
suspicious...
The ability to focus is a gift you
possess, but right now it possesses
you. Scatter your energies more and
chase the many goals of your life—
We know you have a dozen of them...
Do you wish to end this incarnation
having missed out on the eleven things
you might have achieved because you
chased only after the one you cannot
have? Throw your love to the wind
and let your energies find their own
home...
We will be here to help point out
the path, but you must walk it
yourself.

Though I have no idea what the "Garden episode" was, I have always believed that the one I "cannot have" may be children. After another two miscarriages I have seen the wisdom in my Higher Self's admonitions. I returned to school to pursue my master's degree, began writing again, and, as was suggested, began seeking the other goals I had for my life which had been shelved for several years. I am now confident I can fulfill my life in other ways, and I am much happier than I was when I was baby-obsessed.

Be prepared for anything when you communicate with your Higher Self, even a sense of humor in commenting on things that may seem tragically important to you which are not really that intense in the greater scheme of things. Often I have had some little crisis in my life put in perspective by a frustratingly non-serious Higher Self.

If you wish to know about your past lives, the Higher Self is an excellent source for gleaning information. Automatic Writing will not provide you with the clear, precise pictures that past-life regression can provide, but they can be very useful in gaining other insights, such as the overall meaning of the lifetime in question, what lessons remain to be learned from it, and who you know in this life who played an active role in that life.

Here is an excerpt from such a communication.

> As to the Polynesian life you
> must understand that you are not
> that person NOW. You no longer bear
> her guilt. There was no fault.
> What happened is done with. Let
> yourself overcome those old
> superstitions which bound you...
> The boy left behind is who you

think it is, but he bears you
no grudge. Forgive yourself as
he forgives you...

Sometimes your Higher Self acts as your common sense when you either become confused about an issue or begin to lose your objectivity. When I began graduate school I thought I was prepared for the vast workload I would acquire, but by mid-semester the reality of it became overwhelming when placed in the context of all the obligations I had, and I feared I would would start falling behind. Worst of all, I was a commuter student living an hour away from the campus, and I was growing angry about my wasted two hours of driving each day. I was trying to sort out my crowded life with Automatic Writing when my Higher Self suggested to me the most obvious and practical way to use that time—put my notes on tape as I studied so I could play them back to myself as I commuted. This is an excerpt from that communication:

You aren't thinking clearly anymore.
You don't get enough rest and you
worry so much about getting everything
done that less and less is getting
accomplished. If you weren't in
school and wanted to learn something

while you were driving what would you
do? You'd put the information on tape...

Feel free to ask your Higher Self about anything. You cannot offend it. It is part of you, and
living your life without it is as silly as trying to live
your life without an arm or leg if one had been
provided to you. It plays many roles in your life:
counselor, teacher, advisor, helper, and friend.

A Story of The Helpful Higher Self

Janet and her friends often engaged in psychic
experiments just for fun. The current interest is
in Automatic Writing which they had been practicing for some time. They always enjoyed com-
paring messages they received while working
together.

On this Saturday afternoon Janet had left her
husband, Jeff, home in bed asleep, and was with
her friends at a house across town where they
were doing Automatic Writing together. She was
looking forward to a relaxing evening with her
friends; Jeff was scheduled to work an evening
shift which would start in another hour or so, and
she didn't feel like sitting home alone all night.

As was her norm, she began her writing by
contacting her Higher Self and immediately
received the urgent message:

Jeff is still asleep!

Janet pulled the pen from the paper and stared at the single line of communication. Jeff should not only be up by now, she thought, but already on his way to work. If he was late, or didn't show up, his boss would not take it well. In fact, she knew tardiness could cost him his job.

She stared at the page for another minute or so wondering what to do. She'd feel really foolish if she raced off for the phone, upset everyone around her, and then find no answer on the other end, but on the other hand, if Jeff really was over-sleeping she knew she had to wake him.

Quietly, Janet went into the kitchen and called home. Sure enough, Jeff's sleepy voice answered. His alarm clock had not gone off. If he rushed, he could still get to work on time.

While Janet knows the success of this communication was insignificant in comparison to a situation she had heard of in which an Automatic Writer was warned of imminent danger and was able to rush in and save a life, she is still glad for the time she was able to help save her husband's job by knowing when to wake him.

Entities You Can Contact

Type of Entity	Ease of Contact	Reliability of Information
Higher Self	Very Easy	Very. Its omniscience is only limited by human interference.
Spirit Guides	Very Easy	Very, but they may withhold crucial information if they deem you should not have it at this time.
Human Discarnates	Some Difficulty	Depends on the type of person he/she was and how much he/she really knows about the issue/ question being asked.
Living Beings	Difficult	Depends on the type of people you are dealing with, how much they want you to know about themselves, what sort of psychic defenses they employ, and if you are prying where you shouldn't.
Elementals; Non-Human Discarnates	Moderately Easy	Very unreliable and unsafe.
Deities	Impossible	N/A

Spirit Guides

Spirit Guides are discarnate entities, both human and non-human, who are charged with the task of assisting living beings through the trials of their lives. There are many different interpretations of what these beings are. Some say they are angels, and in some ways they might be compared to the idea of a Guardian Angel. Others say they are a part of your own soul family, and still others claim them to be former loved ones who chose to help you through this life.

Like the Higher Self, Spirit Guides can only communicate with you through meditations, dreams, or divinations and they have access to the various levels of information present in the collective unconscious. They are not completely infallible in their judgments, but they rarely make mistakes, and they have a deep sense of what you should and should not be told at any given time. Your best interest is their chief concern and they will usually provide you with ample warning of impending difficulties. However, they view your life from an omniscient viewpoint which not even your Higher Mind can achieve, and they may not warn you about all the things your Higher Self will. The Higher Self is part of you and as interested as your conscious mind in self-preservation. A Spirit Guide may let you wander into trouble because s/he feels you need the experience or to learn a lesson unhindered.

Because Spirit Guides are sentient beings they can occasionally break into your communication with other entities. If they do this it is nothing to fear, but a good sign that they are on the job and you have a clear channel to them. Most communication with these entities is intensely personal and you will likely not want to share them with anyone else. Spirit Guides can be brutally honest at times and will not spare your feelings.

If you are interested in meeting one or more of your Spirit Guides face to face in meditations or astral projection, Automatic Writing will help open those doors for you, and even provide you with a way for them to tell you how best to accomplish this.

For example, my husband, Mark, has been toying for years with the idea of making a major career change and his Tarot cards were not providing enough specific information about the concerns he had over many of the details swarming around in his head. He asked me to do an Automatic Writing to glean some guidance from my own Higher Self. He sat next to me during the exercise, his right hand in my left. Though this made it a bit harder for me to get into the needed frame of mind, I did manage, and I ended up contacting his previously unknown Spirit Guide. The communication was full of good advice, ideas he needed to think about before making a decision.

Needless to say, after the introductions had been made, Mark was intrigued and wished to further communicate with his Guide. Having little interest in learning Automatic Writing for himself, he asked me to do it again for him and ask his Spirit Guide how best to contact him. The following is a part of that reading.

> ...Though you are unaware of my
> presence I am with you in all your
> endeavors. I watch you frequently at
> your Astral Residence [a version of
> the popular Astral Temple] though you
> never look for me...
> Build another room onto your Astral
> Home and dedicate it to our work.
> When you are ready, you need only
> go there and call my name...

Another Career Aided By the Spirit Guide

Brad was a junior high school teacher who had grown disillusioned with the modern education system. He had gone into teaching because it was something he really wanted to do and he hoped to make a difference in the lives of the kids in his charge. But the politics of the public schools burned him out in less than ten years and he longed to make a meaningful change in his life. The problem was how to begin. What skills did he have that were marketable? What sort of salary could an ex-teacher realistically expect? Would he be sorry in the long run if he made this move?

Brad turned to his Automatic Writing to help him put things in perspective. He contacted his Spirit Guide, who helped him list all his skills, even the ones he hadn't really thought about as assets. For one, he was reminded that he was bilingual, an excellent asset when living in the Southwest, as he did. He was also reminded that, though he had no degree in computer science, he did have excellent skills with several different computer systems.

All this was encouraging, but Brad was still unsure where all this might lead him without having to return to school for more long years of study. Finally, his Spirit Guide told him to keep his ears open in the "most unlikely place."

A week later Brad felt baffled because he still had no idea where to turn for another job, and he was feeling that frustration when he wandered into his favorite computer store to relax and see what was new. The store manager greeted him by name. Brad was a regular customer. After they spoke for a while about some new software that was in, the manager had to excuse himself to take a phone call. Because the phone was nearby Brad was able to hear the gist of the conversation. Yes, the manager had looked at the phone caller's application. No, he had not yet made a decision.

Brad was interested. Though he was sure no sales job would pay him enough to live on, he thought it was worth asking about. It turned out that the manager was looking for someone to install computer systems for both home and business customers, and to teach the buyers how to run the systems. The person hired would have to be on hand for long-term support for the customer.

Suddenly Brad was glad he had asked. His ears had been open in an unlikely place. He told the manager he would like to apply for the position.

Brad was hired on the spot. He now uses his computer knowledge in a satisfying, fun way, and still uses his teaching skills to help others learn the computer. Living in Texas, his bilingualism makes him flexible and independent. Brad's Spirit Guide was right all along.

Deceased Friends and Relatives

Often New Age thinkers who firmly believe in the concept of reincarnation scoff at the idea of the living being able to contact the spirits of the dead because they are living on in other bodies. Whether that is true or not is immaterial to contacting them. One's spirit is eternal, and the energy that made them in one incarnation still exists. The science of physics has long ago proven that matter—which should include the essence that is a life—cannot be created or destroyed, it can only change forms.

The memories, energy, and soul matter that was your passed over loved one may have merged with a collective soul group, with the collective unconscious, or even transmigrated into another human body, but his or her Higher Self remains and it is that which you can contact through Automatic Writing.

While deceased loved ones will often have your best interest at heart, keep in mind that they are no more reliable in death than they were in life. Your wayward brother who was a pathological liar in life will likely still lie to you from the spirit world.

Also keep in mind that the exact transformation that occurs to us in death is still the great unknown, and we have no way of knowing whether or not we remain intact as individuals or whether we blend with others who share our soul matter, or even if we become a part of one great whole. All these factors can contribute to cloudy writing from these family members and friends.

On the other hand, there is rarely a feeling as joyful as that sensation that you have broken across the greatest barrier which separates one human being from another by receiving a final message or farewell from someone you care about deeply in life.

My maternal grandmother, whom I affectionately knew as "Granny," was very close to me. She was one of those people I could talk to about practically anything. We could laugh together, shop together, play games, and we shared a similar sense of humor. Just as often as I went to her for advice, she would come to me even though I was fifty-five years her junior. She lived well and actively until I was nearly thirty. Immediately after her passing I was acutely aware of her spirit presence near me. Even after she moved away from the earth plane I still would hear her voice, clear and unmistakable, calling my name as I was drifting off to sleep.

She was always fascinated with the occult, and even had a brief fling with Spiritualism in the 1920s. In any case, I knew she was trying to communicate with me, that she wished to speak with me again.

For some time I limited my contact to the dream/astral world until one day when I finally got brave enough to attempt to contact her through Automatic Writing. To my surprise the contact was made quickly and easily. Being the born skeptic I am, I immediately began searching for evidence that the energy moving my hand was indeed from my beloved Granny.

I asked her to tell me something only she would know, and she complied by reciting the details of several experiences we shared, but I was suspicious that maybe these were things which my own subconscious was projecting. Then she told me an anecdote about my mother's childhood, something I had never before known. When I checked the information with my mother I found it to be accurate in every detail.

Human Discarnates Unknown to You

You may also want to attempt to contact other deceased individuals you did not know in life, even those whose life span did not overlap your own. These are often harder to achieve, but many people struggle to do so, feeling there is benefit to be had from it. Popular figures often sought in Automatic Writing are usually famous spiritual teachers such as Edgar Cayce (a famous American psychic from the 1950s), Houdini, Mahatma Ghandi, Jesus, Moses, Buddha, Aleister Crowley (a famous British magician), Dion Fortune (a Pagan teacher and writer), and various saints.

Of course many people enjoy playing with this oracle and wish to contact other popular figures such as Elvis or President Kennedy, but most of these communications leave a lot to be desired and there is reason to doubt their authenticity. If this sort of thing is something that would interest you, do it for the sheer fun of it and do not expect profound spiritual teachings from them.

A Story of Unknown Spirit Contact

When I was fourteen Diana was almost twenty. She was one of the first people I knew who was involved with magick and mysticism. Her driving passion in life was parapsychology, and she had had numerous experiences in spirit contact which both intrigued and frightened me. Most difficult to forget was her first experience, which came as much of a surprise to her as to anyone she later related these events.

When Diana was no more than fourteen herself, she used her Ouija™ board to make contact with spirits—or at least that's what she tried to do. She had had no success with her efforts. No matter how hard she tried to focus on the planchette, it never moved so much as a millimeter. Then, one night, it not only moved, but nearly jumped out of her hands. The letters it spelled out were incomprehensible to her. In sheer frustration she cried, "Speak English!"

Immediately the board began to spell over and over again, WRITE, WRITE, WRITE...

Diana was fascinated. She set the board aside and got out a pen and paper. No sooner did she sit down at her bedroom desk with it than the pen took off on its own spelling out the plea, HELP ME.

Diana engaged the entity in conversation:

Diana: Who are you?
Entity: My name is Alex.
Diana: Why are you here?
Entity: I am lost.
Diana: Where do you want to go?
Entity: I want to find my family.

She asked him how she could help and the communication grew fuzzy once more. Alex said he was not only lost, but bleeding. Diana was partly convinced by then that she had tapped into something currently happening and feared someone in her neighborhood might be being murdered. Admirably keeping her wits about her, she asked him to tell her what he knew about himself, and allowed him free rein to write through her. The story the young spirit revealed was astonishing.

Entity: I am the Grand Duke Alexis Nicholaivich Romanov, son of the Tsar of all the Russias. I bled to death and now I am lost. I want to

find my family. They were with me
when I died, but when I woke up I
was alone.

At age fourteen Diana had never heard of the
Romanovs of Russia, the last royal family of that
country whose members were assassinated during
the Revolution of 1917, and the popular book
Nicholas and Alexandra which chronicled their
lives was not due out for several more years. She
was most intrigued by the fact that she had finally
contacted a ghost, not by the fact that he claimed
to be a prince of some sort. Loathe to give up the
communication, she kept him writing.

Diana: When did you die?
Entity: When the White Army was
  defeated.
Diana: What year?
Entity: 1917, I think. Things
  happened so fast.
Diana: How did you die?
Entity: They shot us all. We were
  very surprised. My father said
  they would let us leave the country.
Diana: Who did they shoot?
Entity: My parents, my sisters, and me.
Diana: Who shot you?
Entity: I couldn't see. My mother
  always worried about my sickness.

> She tried to protect me. She stood
> in front of me so I could not see
> the guns, but I heard them. When I
> woke up I was alone. Can you help me?

Diana did her best to advise the young Tsar to head for a bright light—the standard answer to such a plea for help—but she lost contact with Alex before she knew if he was successful or not.

It was years later, when the famous book about the Romanovs was published, that Diana had a chance to check out her facts. Indeed the little Grand Duke's name was Alexis, and he certainly had been "sick." He suffered from the bleeding disease known as hemophilia. He was killed by gunshot along with his family, and most certainly would have bled to death with his illness. Some accounts say that Alexis' mother, the Tsarina Alexandra, did try in vain to shield her son in those last seconds of their lives. Diana also discovered that the Tsarina was a granddaughter of England's late Queen Victoria, and an Anglophile obsessed with all things English. Not only was she fluent in the language, but she saw to it that her children were also, therefore it was not surprising that Alexis would be able to write in English.

All these facts were unknown to fourteen-year-old Diana, nor could she ever recall any situation where she might have come across those details previously. She only hoped that the lost young man finally found the family he had been separated from for so long.

After this experience Diana never went back to her Ouija™ board, but always used Automatic Writing to contact her spirit friends.

Communicating With the Living

Since all our thoughts, experiences and energy are tied up in the Collective Unconscious, you can indeed communicate with a living being's super-conscious mind through Automatic Writing. People who use the controversial Ouija™ board have been doing this very thing for a long time.

You need to be aware that, in Automatic Writing, this is a difficult connection to make and it usually comes spontaneously, having first been initiated by the other living person's own subconscious or Higher Self. Likewise, contacting a living person known to you is much easier than making a link with someone you do not know. So if you're indulging fantasies of meaningful spiritual contact with some superstar, you are likely to have your dreams crushed.

If your intention in contacting the unconscious mind of someone else is to spy, snoop, or pry you will be sadly disappointed. That person's

Higher Self will likely block or censor any communication which it feels is not in the best interest of that person.

There are many times, though, when such a communication tool may be useful. For example, if someone you wish to talk to is comatose, or too ill to speak, and you wish to find out what you can do for them to make them better, Automatic Writing may be the only way to find out.

A Mother Talks to Her Daughter

Lupe was always close to her daughter, Blanca, an anthropologist currently on sabbatical in South America where she was spending a year doing research with her husband who shared her work. Lupe was proud of her child, who had gotten a doctorate and now taught at a major university. She was even more thrilled to learn that she would soon be a grandmother, though she was saddened that Blanca was so far away as her time drew near.

Lupe was sound asleep one night when she was startled awake by what sounded like her window opening. Paralyzed by fear, she waited anxiously to see the face of the intruder. As she came fully awake she realized that, though she could clearly heard the sound of the window opening, the sash remained firmly shut. A vaporous figure appeared in the room and moved slowly across to the closet.

Then the figure slowly began to take shape. It was Blanca! Lupe's heart went to her throat. Had her beloved child died? This had to be a ghost.

Gathering her wits, Lupe spoke to the apparition. "Blanca, is that you? What is wrong?"

Blanca's shadowy form seemed to make gestures and her mouth moved, but the frustrated mother could make no sense of them.

Moving on shaky legs to her writing table, Lupe tried to calm herself enough to get into a meditative state of mind. She hoped she could communicate with her daughter through Automatic Writing.

> It hurts, Mama, it hurts. I
> wish you were here. The baby is
> coming hard. I am in the
> remote mountains and the medical
> facilities are not the best. I
> am scared, Mama.

Lupe breathed a sigh of relief. Though Blanca was in primitive conditions, she was a strong girl and she would be alright.

Later the next day Lupe received a wire from her son-in-law telling her that she had a new granddaughter and that Blanca was very tired, but otherwise fine.

Neither Lupe's daughter, nor her son-in-law, ever mentioned the midnight communication, which was likely unknown to them. It had probably been initiated by Blanca's own deep fears, during which she reached out over the miles to the greatest source of comfort she knew ... her mother.

Other Discarnates

Other discarnates include beings who are not whole and complete as we think of them. They include beings who are mere fragments of energy, projected astral imprints, elementals, and other non-human spirits which are often as varied as the human psyche. Most of these creatures do not have the power to break through your protective barriers and communicate with you through Automatic Writing, and it is doubtful that they would have anything profound to tell you anyway.

One way to know if one of these beings has "taken over" is when you get facetious, capricious, or silly communications. These creatures love to play games and immensely enjoy this type of nonsense, but they will usually not deliberately try to hurt you.

If you really want to commune with these beings, there are easier and safer ways to do so, but the techniques involved lie outside the scope of this work. Suffice it to say that it is wise not to open a physical channel to them, and, if you feel one has been accidentally made, to shut it down as soon as possible.

Contacting Deities

Repeated tries at contacting the energies of Goddesses and Gods through Automatic Writing have remained unsuccessful. Those who have tried have found their queries unanswered, or else felt them to be responded to by beings they perceived to be Angels, Spirit Guides, or some other guardian spirit depending on the religious and/or cultural background of the writer.

Why deities who live vividly in our minds cannot be projected onto paper is uncertain, though one of the best answers to this perplexing question may be that we secretly do not want our all-powerful deities to be able to communicate with us in this way.

Of course, there is also the possibility that we human beings, at this stage of our development, are simply not able to channel such vast stores of energy.

If you wish to contact your deities, do a ritual, an evocation, or pray.

About Negative Entities and Abusive Language

Sometimes, without inviting it, a negative entity or energy becomes attracted to your Automatic Writing and will break through your protective perimeters. There are ways to determine if this has happened to you, the best way being by the type of language used in the communication. (See the list on the opposite page.)

Though you will rarely, if ever, encounter coercive or abusive Automatic Writing the possibility remains and must be dealt with accordingly. Such writings are easy to distinguish as their root purpose is clearly to seek to harm you or others. Communication that attempts to force you to do something against your will or your ethics, or which demeans and/or degrades you and/or others should be shut off immediately. This should be your first sign that you are not receiving a communication from a loving and highly evolved being and it would be dangerous to continue to play with an obviously malevolent force. Shut down the channel immediately!

Vulgar or coarse language is also rarely encountered, but this a different matter altogether. While such language might be considered by some to be obscene and inappropriate, it isn't going to harm you in and of itself. For instance, if you are seeking to contact the spirit of a randy old

Signs that You have Contacted a Negative Energy/Entity

- Sentences are erratic and confused to the point of being bizarre.

- Drawings you feel compelled to sketch contain disturbing or violent imagery.

- Language is abusive, threatening, or demanding.

- There are demands made that you spend large portions of your time with Automatic Writing.

- There is an obvious attempt to coerce or threaten you into pursuing the negative contact.

- You are asked to do something you do not wish to do, or which goes strongly against your personal ethics.

- Your greatest fears are played upon as a means of forcing you to go against your wishes.

- Guilt tactics and emotional blackmail are evident.

- Your deities, religion, and/or personal ethics are repeatedly denigrated or vilified.

- Extreme cruelty is part of the communication. For example, you are falsely told that a loved one has just died.

uncle who, in life, could not speak one complete sentence without offending someone, then this is quite likely how he will continue to communicate in death. Remember, being dead doesn't necessarily raise one's ideals or morals. If you find you do not care for a message peppered with colorful (or off-color) phrases, you can request that the entity refrain from writing that way, ask to communicate with someone else, or stop the process altogether.

Remember, you are always in control!

❧ 4 ❧

Fine Tuning Your Writing With Astrology

People have used the power of the planets for thousands of years to help align themselves with helpful energies and to tap the fullness of their potential. You can also harness the power of planetary energies to get started with your Automatic Writing, or for fine tuning your explorations to specific questions by deliberately aligning yourself with specific astrological influences.

Each planet has certain energies that are compatible with events in our lives. The best time to use a divinatory tool is when you need it the most, but if you can wait for a favorable astrological period, your success will be greater and your answers clearer and more precise.

How a Lonely Woman Used Astrology to Aid Her Automatic Writing

Lianna was thirty, unmarried, and likely to stay that way. A bad relationship with a young man ten years earlier had left her distrustful of men and romance. Every time she thought she had finally met someone wonderful, she would feel compelled to do something to discourage his attentions, and each time she would tell herself it was just as well, that it probably would not have worked out for her anyway. Needless to say, after ten years of this destructive behavior, Lianna's self-esteem was almost non-existent.

One of her great interests was metaphysics, and she had only recently learned how to do Automatic Writing. She really wanted to ask her Higher Self about her romantic problems, but she was having trouble getting clear answers to her inquiries. Finally she decided the only way to change that was to align herself as strongly as possible with all the astrological influences that might help her succeed.

Lianna chose Venus, the planet associated with romantic love, as the one she needed to work with in order to get better answers to her problem. She decided to bathe her work area in a pale green light (a Venusian color), found pale green writing paper, and bought a green felt-tipped pen. She wanted to do her writing on a full moon, on a Friday, Venus' day, and wait until the moon was in Taurus (a sign ruled by Venus), but in order to have all these influences coincide, she would have to wait almost six months. She decided to make do with what she had. She chose a Friday when the moon was in Cancer (a sign of home life), when the moon was waxing and almost full.

At the time she chose to work she made the sigil of Venus on the top of her writing paper, all the while trying to sense the essence of the planet within the marks she made. Then she turned on her green lights, and even lit a few green candles for good measure, then sat down where she would be working, and took herself into a meditative state. Before she opened her eyes to write she spent a few minutes focusing on the qualities of Venus, allowing them to enter her Crown Chakra and merge their energy with her own.

Then she opened her eyes and waited for the needed message from her Higher Self. She was surprised that the words seemed to flow so easily from her pen:

> You must open the doors of your heart
> and shut the one on fear. I do not
> have to tell you this. You have known
> it all along. It is an ancient wisdom
> that in order to receive love we must
> first allow ourselves to give love.
> For whatever reason you needed to have
> this said to you. But only you can act
> upon it. Only you can change your
> life. No one can promise that you

will not be hurt again in the process,
but is that really so awful when
compared to the ultimate prize you
seek?

By the time Lianna finished writing she was
in tears. Her Higher Self was right, this piece of
wisdom was not news to her, it was only common
sense. But for whatever reason, once the words
were written out in front of her, they penetrated
to the surface of her consciousness where they
could be acted upon.

By aligning her own energies with that of
Venus, Lianna finally got a clear Automatic Writing, one she desperately needed to have. The
flood gates to her subconscious were flung open,
and all her Automatic Writings—and her life in
general—became easier.

The Power of the Planets

The first, and easiest way, to harness planetary
energy is according to the day of the week. Each
of the seven major planets governs one day, a
twenty-four hour period during which its influence is most keenly felt. In the Romance languages of Europe, the days of the week refer to
the planets (i.e.; Mardi is French for the "day of
Mars," and Mercredi is the "day of Mercury," etc.).

This is what they are in English:

Sunday	Sun
Monday	Moon
Tuesday	Mars
Wednesday	Mercury
Thursday	Jupiter
Friday	Venus
Saturday	Saturn

Each planet has its own meanings, influences, traditional associations, and arenas which it governs:

SUN—protection, employment, strength, leadership, men, royalty, display, theater, entertainment/performing arts, heat, charity, volunteering, government, law, the God, prosperity, self-confidence, movement/dance, fire, power, self-defense, spiritual attainment, the day, purification, public matters, and exorcism.

MOON—fertility, motherhood, childbirth, psychicism, women, the Goddess, life cycles, dreams, growth, astral projection, the subconscious, spirituality, water, sleep, reincarnation, private matters, the night, the home, animals, peace, tranquility, nursing, the elements and elementals.

MARS—war, sex/lust, courage, banishing, medicine, passion, the military, aggression, strife, fear, police/soldiers, combat, disagreement, physical exertion, competition, group power, anger, group strength, machinery, carpentry, bargaining power, and needle crafts.

MERCURY—communication, healing, herbalism, writing, wisdom, mental prowess/ intellect, books, reading, gossip, vocal music, travel, correspondence, diplomacy, mathematics, the sciences, history, school/education, mass media, visiting, libraries, teachers, and students.

JUPITER—money, employment, prosperity, good fortune, fair judgments, friendship, investments, ambition, wealth, prestige, success, courtrooms, gambling, foreign interests, astronomy, social events, long travels, publishing, research, psychology, clergy, and self-improvement.

VENUS—family, husbands/wives, sweethearts, love/romance, peace, fashion, architecture, sewing, light amusements, dating, intimate social gatherings, shopping, close friendships, gardening, fidelity, emotions, music, home life, children, pets, acts of kindness and generosity, art, poetry, and beauty.

SATURN—past-life recall, self-undoing, lies, mental and emotional distress, losses, the elderly, completion, spirit communication, repairs, excavations, archaeology, death, structure, reality, morality, meditation, accepting or changing bad situations, and protection from psychic attack.

For example, if you want to get started with Automatic Writing, you may wish to begin on a Monday to gather the psychic powers of the moon, or on a Sunday which is associated with action and success.

Mercury in Retrograde

A planet is said to be in retrograde when, from the perspective of the earth, it appears to be traveling backwards in its orbit. Of course, this is not really the case, it is merely an optical illusion, but one which astrologically affects us here on earth.

Mercury goes through approximately three periods of retrograde each calendar year, and since it is the planet that governs communication it is one which has a profound effect on Automatic Writing. These periods can last for several weeks during which you should be on the lookout for misunderstandings in your Automatic Writing. You will probably experience a greater amount of cryptic, or even garbled, messages.

The Planetary Hours

Another more precise way to harness these energies is by calculating the planetary hours of the day, each of which are ruled by a different planet whose influence can be felt or tapped at that time. This system of figuring the planetary hours dates back to the early medieval period. It divides the hours of daylight and the hours of darkness each into twelve divisions. Since there are twenty-four hours in every day, when we are at either the spring or autumn equinox every planet has exactly two hours of influence.

To calculate these times for yourself, you will need a chart of sunrise and sunset times. (These can be obtained through local weather services, departments of fish and game, or from a local synagogue where these charts are kept handy to calculate the starting and stopping times of their holidays based on these times.) Take the total number of hours and minutes of daylight and divide by twelve. This will tell you exactly how long each planetary hour will be. Likewise, take the total number of hours and minutes of darkness, and divide by twelve and you will get the length of each planetary hour of the night.

Next, look to the "Planetary Hours Chart" and see which planet governs each hour. For example, if you are doing an Automatic Writing about money during the daylight on a Sunday and want to add the influence of Jupiter, which governs money matters, you would want to write during the sixth planetary hour of the day.

It is certainly not necessary to use this elaborate system in divination, but if you are having problems of any kind, these subtle energies can give you the boost you may need for success.

The Mother Moon

Aside from the sun which gives us light and warmth and shows us the basis of our personalities, the planet which exerts the most profound psychic influence on us is our neighbor, the moon. Since before recorded time human beings have been working with the cycles of the moon when planting, picking, growing, beginning or ending projects. The best time to begin your sixty- day practice of Automatic Writing is during the waxing phase of the moon, preferably during the second quarter. This helps you harness the psychic power associated with the full moon as well as the growing and expanding energies of the moon's growth phase.

In relating the moon's cycles to specific questions, matters relating to increase or gain can be best asked when the moon is waxing, and matters relating to decrease or loss are best dealt with when the moon is on the wane.

The Plan

Daylight Hours

Sunday	Monday	Tuesday	Wednesday
1. Sun	Moon	Mars	Mercury
2 Venus	Saturn	Sun	Moon
3 Mercury	Jupiter	Venus	Saturn
4 Moon	Mars	Mercury	Jupiter
5 Saturn	Sun	Moon	Mars
6 Jupiter	Venus	Saturn	Sun
7 Mars	Mercury	Jupiter	Venus
8 Sun	Moon	Mars	Mercury
9 Venus	Saturn	Sun	Moon
10 Mercury	Jupiter	Venus	Saturn
11 Moon	Mars	Mercury	Jupiter
12 Saturn	Sun	Moon	Mars

Nighttime Hours

Sunday	Monday	Tuesday	Wednesday
1 Jupiter	Venus	Saturn	Sun
2 Mars	Mercury	Jupiter	Venus
3 Sun	Moon	Mars	Mercury
4 Venus	Saturn	Sun	Moon
5 Mercury	Jupiter	Venus	Saturn
6 Moon	Mars	Mercury	Jupiter
7 Saturn	Sun	Moon	Mars
8 Jupiter	Venus	Saturn	Sun
9 Mars	Mercury	Jupiter	Venus
10 Sun	Moon	Mars	Mercury
11 Venus	Saturn	Sun	Moon
12 Mercury	Jupiter	Venus	Saturn

ary Hours

Thursday	Friday	Saturday
Jupiter	Venus	Saturn
Mars	Mercury	Jupiter
Sun	Moon	Mars
Venus	Saturn	Sun
Mercury	Jupiter	Venus
Moon	Mars	Mercury
Saturn	Sun	Moon
Jupiter	Venus	Saturn
Mars	Mercury	Jupiter
Sun	Moon	Mars
Venus	Saturn	Sun
Mercury	Jupiter	Venus

Thursday	Friday	Saturday
Moon	Mars	Mercury
Saturn	Sun	Moon
Jupiter	Venus	Saturn
Mars	Mercury	Jupiter
Sun	Moon	Mars
Venus	Saturn	Sun
Mercury	Jupiter	Venus
Moon	Mars	Mercury
Saturn	Sun	Moon
Jupiter	Venus	Saturn
Mars	Mercury	Jupiter
Sun	Moon	Mars

The moon travels in and out of the twelve signs of the zodiac about every twenty-eight days, just short of a full lunar month (twenty-nine and a half days). When the moon is in each of these signs its influence is affected and shaped accordingly, and certain signs are better for starting Automatic Writing than others, and others are best for doing divinatory work in general.

MOON IN ARIES—Aries is a barren sign, and not an auspicious beginning for any inner-plane endeavor. If you are having trouble getting started with Automatic Writing, avoid beginning again when the moon is in Aries. This may be hard to do as Aries tends to make us enthusiastic to begin new projects. Force yourself to turn your attention to physical labors, purge yourself with work, and begin your writing when the moon is in a more favorable position.

MOON IN TAURUS—The influence of the moon in Taurus makes us protective and stubborn, and it will affect your psyche by making it loathe to provide you with information it feels might be the least bit upsetting to you. If you are asking about a delicate matter, wait until the moon moves on to deal with it. Taurus is a good time to ask about matters relating to the fine arts.

MOON IN GEMINI—Gemini is the most eclectic of all the signs, but also the most mercurial and fickle. Because the sign is ruled by Mercury, it is an excellent time for any type of communication, though those messages may sometimes appear confused or contradictory. When the moon moves on you can ask for any needed clarification.

MOON IN CANCER—Cancer is the most fertile sign in the zodiac and virtually anything undertaken during this time will grow favorably, especially psychic endeavors, as Cancer is the home of the moon. This is also the best sign for dealing with matters relating to home and children or to the emotions.

MOON IN LEO—In contrast to Cancer, Leo is the most barren sign in the zodiac. You will need to harness all the vibrant energy of the sun, Leo's planet, to make your writing work when begun here. This can be done by planning your writing during times when the sun's influence peaks. Once you are able to do this successfully, Leo is a good time to ask about matters dealing with leadership or money.

MOON IN VIRGO—Virgo is the fastidious intellectual of the zodiac, and when the moon is in Virgo it is a good time to work with matters pertaining to education, volunteerism, and health. It is also a moderately fertile sign and not a bad time to start practicing your Automatic Writing.

MOON IN LIBRA—When the moon is in Libra our minds turn to aesthetics and to balance. It is a good time to ask questions about appearances and justice. Answers received during this transit are often satirical.

MOON IN SCORPIO—Scorpio is the keeper of secrets, and a good time to unlock a few through Automatic Writing. It is also a very fertile sign and a good time to begin learning this art. Matters pertaining to sexuality, deceit, trustworthiness, and things hidden are best dealt with now.

MOON IN SAGITTARIUS—This transit makes us all philosophers and places us in a frame of mind to deal with issues of humanity, peace, and the right way of the universe. Answers received during this time are upbeat and straightforward, and are rarely cryptic.

MOON IN CAPRICORN—This is a time for dealing with material concerns, such as information about obtaining a new car. It is also a time when negative emotions and despondency tend to come to the fore. If you are prone to depression do not use this time to ask questions that are vital to you and whose negative response might upset you all the more.

MOON IN AQUARIUS—There has been a lot of New Age hype about the sterling qualities of Aquarius but, like all the signs, it has its negative aspects. These include things like selfishness, thought without action, and generally allowing one's mind to wander aimlessly in some vast pseudo-intellectual wilderness. However, it is also a time when people as a whole tend to be fairly rational and this will aid you in interpreting your Automatic Writing.

MOON IN PISCES—Second only to Cancer, this is the most fertile of all the signs and an excellent time to begin learning Automatic Writing. It is a time when emotions can become clouded and your writings will show more emotional wanderings than fact, and more hard-to-decode cryptic messages are likely to appear. But it is also a time when psychic sensitivity peaks, making your writing much easier to do.

When the moon has moved out of its last major aspect (a calculated directional relationship) with another planet before moving into another astrological sign it is said to be "void of course." Astrological studies have shown that events undertaken during these hours tend to be difficult if not impossible, and rarely pan out as expected. If you are learning Automatic Writing for the first time, avoid trying to work during the hours when the moon is void of course.

Colors of the Zodiac

Each planet and astrological sign has a color or colors which are associated with it and share its energy qualities. These are very old attributes and, therefore, they carry a great amount of symbolic power and can be used to further attune with the influences you seek.

Zodiac color can be easily added to your Automatic Writing exercises by what you choose to wear, the color of the ink in your pen, or the color of the paper on which you write. You can also use colored candles or light bulbs to flood your work area with the energy of the color and the planet/sign it represents.

Below are listed the planets and signs along with both their traditional astrological colors, and the colors attributed to them by the Judeo-Gnostic mystical system known as Kaballah.

Planet/sign	Basic Color(s)	Kabalistic Color
Sun	Orange, Gold	Yellow
Moon	Silver	Violet
Mercury	Bright Blue, Green	Orange
Venus	Pale Blue, Green	Green
Mars	Scarlet, Maroon	Red
Jupiter	Blue-Green	Blue
Saturn	Black	Black
Aries	Red	Red
Taurus	Pastels	Red-Orange
Gemini	Pale Yellow	Orange
Cancer	Silver, Green	Orange-Yellow
Leo	Orange, Gold	Yellow
Virgo	Dark Blue	Yellow-Green
Libra	Pink	Green
Scorpio	Dark Yellow	Green-Blue
Sagittarius	Indigo	Blue
Capricorn	Brown, Forest	Indigo
Aquarius	Bright Blue	Violet
Pisces	Sea Green, Silver	Red-Violet

Another way to direct the energy of the zodiac is by making a Zodiac Wand. These have been favorite magickal tools in some circles for a long time because they are easy to construct and to use. After all, what item is more linked in the popular mind with magick than a wand?

The idea behind the Zodiac Wand is to have all the astrological signs and their colors equally represented, along with a space at either end that you design yourself to represent both spirit and matter. The colors, when properly mixed, will visually appear to flow into one another, their energies and essences blurring and combining, just as the energy you are drawing down will do. For Automatic Writing, or for any other magickal/ psychic operation, the wand is grasped with one hand by the sign you wish to align yourself with. The end representing spirit is held upward and the end representing matter is pointed down. By concentrating on the wand as a catalyst for directing energy you can effectively channel down the astrological influence you need from the world of spirit to that of matter where it can be of use to you. The more you use the wand for this purpose, the more of your personal energy it will absorb, and the stronger a tool it will become for you.

To begin you will need to have on hand sandpaper and one three-foot wooden dowel rod that is about one inch in diameter. These dowels are easy and inexpensive to obtain at any hardware or craft store. With your sandpaper, slightly round the ends of the dowel so that it has smooth edges. This is so that the energy you are going to channel through it will encounter no harsh corners and will be allowed to flow smoothly to where you need it to be.

Next you will need to take a ruler and carefully measure off the sections of the dowel. Starting from either end, mark off four and a half inches. From that point on, mark off twelve spaces of two and a quarter inches each. When you reach the other end you should be left with a space four and a half inches long.

When you are satisfied that you have your wand marked off as accurately as possible it will be time to paint it. For painting you will need seven small bottles of acrylic paint: red, orange, yellow, green, blue, purple, and black. From these colors all the others you will need can be mixed. Starting at either end you choose, begin painting the two-and-a-quarter inch spaces starting with red and moving down the following list:

Red (Aries)
Red-Orange (Taurus)
Orange (Gemini)
Orange-Yellow (Cancer)
Yellow (Leo)
Yellow-Green (Virgo)
Green (Libra)
Green-Blue (Scorpio)
Blue (Sagittarius)

Indigo (Capricorn)
Violet (Aquarius)
Red-Violet (Pisces)

You can mix all the combination colors yourself in a small glass jar or mug until you have found the shade you want.

Allow the wand to dry in a safe place.

After the paint has dried, take a thin detail paint brush and the black paint and, in the center of the color, paint on the sigil that represents each sign (See "Symbols of the Zodiac" on Page 90).

For the two four-and-a-half-inch end areas, you may design them according to personal taste. All that matters is that they represent spirit and matter to you. The end next to Aries (the first sign of the zodiac) will be designated SPIRIT and the end near Pisces (the last sign of the zodiac) will be designated MATTER.

On my wand I have spirit painted white and matter black, though some persons prefer to reverse the two. You can also use silver paint for spirit and brown for matter. Or you can paint the symbol for the Sun on spirit, and the one for earth on matter.

Use your imagination. Draw pictures, create new symbols, or use a variety of colors if you like. What is most important is how it makes you feel.

Making the Zodiac Wand

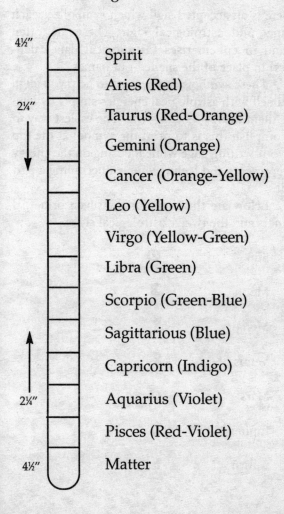

4½"

2¼" ↓

Spirit
Aries (Red)
Taurus (Red-Orange)
Gemini (Orange)
Cancer (Orange-Yellow)
Leo (Yellow)
Virgo (Yellow-Green)
Libra (Green)
Scorpio (Green-Blue)
Sagittarious (Blue)
Capricorn (Indigo)

↑

2¼"

Aquarius (Violet)
Pisces (Red-Violet)

4½"

Matter

Symbols of the Zodiac

There is an accepted sigil which symbolizes each planet and astrological sign. These are often found in ephemerises (astrological data calendars) in place of the spelled-out names.

These symbols can be used to help you align yourself with astrological energies simply by having them nearby as you write. The easiest way to accomplish this is to print the symbol at the top of your writing page while focusing on the energy it represents and feeling yourself becoming a part of it.

Below are the sigils for the seven principal planets and the twelve astrological signs.

Sun	☉
Moon	☽
Mercury	☿
Venus	♀
Mars	♂
Jupiter	♃
Saturn	♄

Aries	♈
Taurus	♉
Gemini	♊
Cancer	♋
Leo	♌
Virgo	♍
Libra	♎
Scorpio	♏
Sagittarius	♐
Capricorn	♑
Aquarius	♒
Pisces	♓

Other Astrological Influences

There are numerous other planetary influences which any astrologer can discuss at length, but which do not greatly influence divination. These are things such as aspects, conjunctions, and planetary alignments.

The Best Times for Automatic Writing

Again, keep in mind that the best time to use any oracle is when you need it, but if you can wait, or feel you need the added boost astrology can offer, then you can use the above information to determine the best times to do your Automatic Writing. Below you will find a guide to help you make your time selection. It is very unlikely that you will find all of these influences working for you at one time unless you are willing to wait many years for them to coincide. If you find you cannot do your writing at the proper planetary hour or during the right moon sign, remember that as far as astrology goes, the phase of the moon and day of the week have the strongest influences over you.

> Asking About Romantic Relationships
> Moon Phase: 1st quarter
> Day of Week: Friday
> Planetary Hour: Venus or Moon
> Moon Sign: Cancer

Issues in a Marriage
  Moon Phase: Any
  Day of the Week: Wednesday
  Planetary Hour: Venus
  Moon Sign: Cancer

Sexual Matters
  Moon Phase: Any
  Day of the Week: Tuesday
  Planetary Hour: Mars or Mercury
  Moon Sign: Aries or Scorpio

Questions About Gaining Employment
  Moon Phase: 1st or 2nd quarter
  Day of the Week: Thursday
  Planetary Hour: Jupiter or Sun
  Moon Sign: Sagittarius

Questions About Ending Employment
  Moon Phase: 3rd or 4th quarter
  Day of the Week: Sunday
  Planetary Hour: Jupiter or Sun
  Moon Sign: Sagittarius

Dealing With Major Disputes/Arbitration
  Moon Phase: 4th quarter
  Day of the Week: Friday
  Planetary Hour: Mars
  Moon Sign: Taurus

Asking Questions About a Personal Quarrel
Moon Phase: 3rd or 4th quarter
Day of the Week: Tuesday
Planetary Hour: Mars
Moon Sign: Aries

Asking About an Enemy
Moon Phase: Dark
Day of the Week: Tuesday
Planetary Hour: Mars or Saturn
Moon Sign: Aries or Leo

Dealing With Gossip/Lies
Moon Phase: 4th quarter
Day of the Week: Saturday
Planetary Hour: Mercury
Moon Sign: Gemini

Issues of Money
Moon Phase: Any
Day of the Week: Sunday
Planetary Hour: Sun
Moon Sign: Leo

For Issues of Personal Protection
Moon Phase: 2nd quarter
Day of the Week: Tuesday
Planetary Hour: Sun or Mars
Moon Sign: Aries

For Issues of Psychic Protection
  Moon Phase: 2nd quarter
  Day of the Week: Monday
  Planetary Hour: Mars, Sun, or Saturn
  Moon Sign: Cancer or Sagittarius

Issues of Personal Appearance/Beauty
  Moon Phase: Any
  Day of the Week: Friday
  Planetary Hour: Venus or Moon
  Moon Sign: Libra or Taurus

Help With Ending a Phobia
  Moon Phase: 4th quarter
  Day of the Week: Tuesday or Saturday
  Planetary Hour: Mars or Sun
  Moon Sign: Virgo

Asking for Suggestions on Spellwork
  Moon Phase: Full
  Day of the Week: Monday
  Planetary Hour: Depends on nature of spell
  Moon Sign: Pisces

Asking for Help to Construct a Ritual
  Moon Phase: 1st quarter
  Day of the Week: Sun or Moon
  Planetary Hour: Mercury
  Moon Sign: Scorpio or Aquarius

Inquiries About the Elderly
  Moon Phase: 3rd or 4th quarter
  Day of the Week: Saturday
  Planetary Hour: Sun
  Moon Sign: Capricorn

Questions of Religion, Morality, Ethics, etc.
  Moon Phase: Any except Dark
  Day of the Week: Sunday
  Planetary Hour: Jupiter
  Moon Sign: Leo, Virgo, or Capricorn

Asking About Astral Travel
  Moon Phase: 1st or 2nd quarter
  Day of the Week: Wednesday
  Planetary Hour: Moon
  Moon Sign: Pisces or Gemini

Asking About Physical Travel
  Moon Phase: 1st or 2nd quarter
  Day of the Week: Wednesday
  Planetary Hour: Mercury
  Moon Sign: Gemini or Virgo

Contacting the Dead
  Moon Phase: Any
  Day of the Week: Monday or Saturday
  Planetary Hour: Moon or Saturn
  Moon Sign: Scorpio or Pisces

Divining the Immediate Future
  Moon Phase: 1st or 2nd quarter
  Day of the Week: Sun
  Planetary Hour: Sun
  Moon Sign: Cancer

Asking About the Far Future
  Moon Phase: Full or early 3rd quarter
  Day of the Week: Monday
  Planetary Hour: Mercury
  Moon Sign: Pisces

Retrieving Information From Past
  Moon Phase: 3rd or 4th quarter
  Day of the Week: Saturday
  Planetary Hour: Mercury or Moon
  Moon Sign: Capricorn

Asking About a Past-Life
  Moon Phase: Any
  Day of the Week: Moon
  Planetary Hour: Saturn
  Moon Sign: Cancer or Scorpio

Asking About Legal Matters
  Moon Phase: Full
  Day of the Week: Sunday
  Planetary Hour: Mercury
  Moon Sign: Libra

Matters Relating to Education
  Moon Phase: Any
  Day of the Week: Wednesday
  Planetary Hour: Mercury
  Moon Sign: Virgo or Aquarius

To Help Clear Up a Misunderstanding
  Moon Phase: Late 4th quarter
  Day of the Week: Wednesday
  Planetary Hour: Mars or Mercury
  Moon Sign: Gemini

To Ask About a Loved One on Military Duty
  Moon Phase: 2nd quarter
  Day of the Week: Saturday
  Planetary Hour: Saturn
  Moon Sign: Aries (if in combat), Virgo (if
    on peace duty)

To Ask About Living, Absent Loved Ones
  Moon Phase: Full
  Day of the Week: Friday
  Planetary Hour: Mercury or Venus
  Moon Sign: Gemini

To Help Locate a Lost Object
  Moon Phase: 2nd quarter
  Day of the Week: Thursday
  Planetary Hour: Moon
  Moon Sign: Libra

Asking About Children
  Moon Phase: Any
  Day of the Week: Friday
  Planetary Hour: Venus or Moon
  Moon Sign: Cancer

General Divination
  Moon Phase: Preferably Waxing
  Day of the Week: Sunday
  Planetary Hour: Sun or Mercury
  Moon Sign: Cancer or Pisces

Dealing With Pregnancy Concerns
  Moon Phase: Full
  Day of the Week: Monday
  Planetary Hour: Moon or Venus
  Moon Sign: Cancer

Questions About Motherhood
  Moon Phase: Full
  Day of the Week: Monday
  Planetary Hour: Mercury
  Moon Sign: Cancer or Virgo

Questions About Fatherhood
  Moon Phase: Any
  Day of the Week: Sunday
  Planetary Hour: Moon
  Moon Sign: Leo or Gemini

To Do a General Reading for Others
  Moon Phase: Any
  Day of the Week: Wednesday
  Planetary Hour: Moon or Venus
  Moon Sign: Virgo or Aquarius

Asking About Social Matters/Clubs
  Moon Phase: 3rd quarter
  Day of the Week: Thursday
  Planetary Hour: Jupiter or Sun
  Moon Sign: Sagittarius

Questions of Health/Healing or Medicine
  Moon Phase: 2nd quarter
  Day of the Week: Sunday or Tuesday
  Planetary Hour: Moon
  Moon Sign: Leo or Aries

Leadership Issues
  Moon Phase: Full
  Day of the Week: Sunday
  Planetary Hour: Sun or Mars
  Moon Sign: Leo

Issues Relating to Government
  Moon Phase: Waning
  Day of the Week: Tuesday
  Planetary Hour: Sun or Mars
  Moon Sign: Aquarius

Matters Related to the Fine Arts
 Moon Phase: 1st quarter
 Day of the Week: Monday
 Planetary Hour: Mercury
 Moon Sign: Pisces or Taurus

Overcoming Creative Blocks (such as
  writer's block)
 Moon Phase: 3rd or 4th quarter
 Day of the Week: Mercury
 Planetary Hour: Venus, Mercury, or Sun
 Moon Sign: Taurus

To Ask About Someone With Whom You've
  Lost Touch
 Moon Phase: 2nd quarter or Full
 Day of the Week: Wednesday
 Planetary Hour: Mercury
 Moon Sign: Virgo or Gemini

Issues of Self-Esteem/Confidence
 Moon Phase: Full
 Day of the Week: Sunday
 Planetary Hour: Jupiter
 Moon Sign: Leo

Help in Banishing a Bad Habit
 Moon Phase: 4th quarter or dark
 Day of the Week: Thursday
 Planetary Hour: Saturn or Jupiter
 Moon Sign: Capricorn

For Help Interpreting a Dream
  Moon Phase: 1st or 2nd quarter, or Full
  Day of the Week: Monday
  Planetary Hour: Moon or Saturn
  Moon Sign: Pisces or Cancer

When You Aren't Sure of the Issue at Hand
  Moon Phase: Full or Dark
  Day of the Week: Monday or Saturday
  Planetary Hour: Moon or Saturn
  Moon Sign: Pisces or Sagittarius

❧ 5 ❧

Preparing Yourself
To Contact Other
Intelligences

My method of facilitating Automatic Writing is
through meditation, and by using the chakra system to channel the needed energy. Therefore, in
order to learn this art you will first need to learn
meditation exercises.

Deep Breathing Exercises and Proper Breathing Technique

Deep breathing has been taught to students of
metaphysics for thousands of years as one of the
most basic tools for self-awareness. Basic deep
breathing is done by drawing air in through your
nose and passing it out through your mouth. This
process has long been believed to set up a powerful energy circuit within the body (i.e.; breath
becomes energy) which benefits not only your
psychic work, but your physical health and well-
being as well.

The reasons for the health benefits are self-evident. The nose contains hair follicles and mucous membranes that filter impurities and germs which seek to enter your lungs. The nose also has the ability to warm the air to nearly body temperature as it passes through, and warmed air is less of a strain on your lungs, particularly if you suffer from asthma or any other respiratory disease that threatens to constrict the air passageways. Those who suffer from digestive problems will also find that proper breathing helps them, as the same muscle that moves the lungs also stimulates the stomach.

Most people find themselves short of breath at times simply because they try to breathe from their chests instead of from deep within the bottom of the lungs. Sometimes this is the natural result of wearing restrictive clothing, and sometimes it is a carry-over of how we were taught as children. When engaged in sports in elementary school or learning how to swim we were often told to "take a deep breath." In the exaggerated way of children, we would throw back our shoulders and puff out our chests to demonstrate our marvelous lung capacity. As these exercises were meant to be for fun, no one ever bothered to correct our mistakes, and they soon became bad habits.

The correct way of breathing is from the diaphragm. The diaphragm is the large elliptical

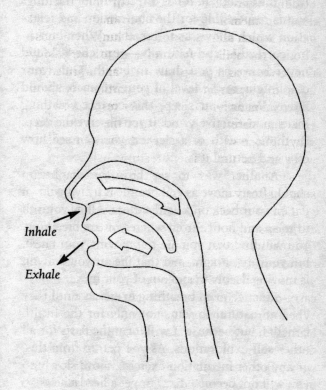

Inhale

Exhale

The Proper Way to Do Deep Breathing

muscle partition that separates the chest cavity from the abdomen. It lies directly under the lungs and is responsible for the contraction and relaxation which allows us to breathe. When breathing correctly—and naturally—your chest should never heave as you draw in breath. Only your diaphragm, at the level of your stomach, should move. When you sleep, this correct breathing kicks in instinctively and, if you observe the deep, rhythmic breath of a sleeper, you can see how easy and natural it is.

Another way to see how the diaphragm should freely move as you breathe is by lying down flat on your back on a hard surface. Allow yourself to relax and notice from where you are breathing. You will find that you are not moving your chest, but your diaphragm, and that the air you draw in is moving deeply in and out of your lungs.

Practice deep breathing exercises until they become natural to you, not only for the health benefits, but because it will form the basis for all other self-explorations. As you get up from this, or any other meditation exercise, move slowly so you will not become dizzy or get a headache.

Discovering Your Prana

From ancient India, where the art of meditation was first perfected, comes the idea of controlled

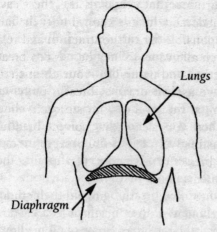

The Diaphragm when inhaling

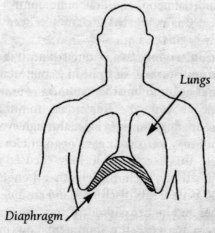

The Diaphragm when exhaling

breathing, sometimes known as the "sacred breath" (prana), which is central to their beliefs about connecting the earth-bound mind to other forms of consciousness. They found that by varying the length and depth of the breath one could attain various levels of conscious and super-conscious awareness. As these ideas spread both to the east and west, and were adopted into the occult practices of various cultures, refinements and changes came to the concept of prana. Today most occult schools of thought advocate some form of controlled breathing to aid their students in the attainment of their magickal goals.

In fact, the most basic type of all meditation is the conscious awareness of one's own breathing patterns and, later on, the deliberate control of them. It is at this point that the study of meditation usually begins.

To begin, simply find a quiet place where you will be undisturbed, sit or lie in a comfortable position, and begin to breathe naturally, counting each exhale as you go. (Remember to inhale through your nose and exhale through your mouth!) You may keep your eyes open or closed. The point of this exercise is to keep focused on your own breathing, excluding all other thoughts.

As you perfect this discipline, and are able to count higher and higher without your mind wandering, begin to sense the imminent power in your own breath. As you inhale try to see your breath as more than a necessary function to sustain life, but rather as a tool for drawing in powerful energies that can be harnessed to aid you as you so direct. Practice visualizing the inhalation of colors or vibrations that you are drawn to, and which you feel might aid you in your ultimate goal. Inhale a silver light to aid in psychic work, a vivid purple to speed healing, or a bright yellow to aid in communication. Begin to think of your breath as a practical tool for spiritual growth rather than an involuntary physiological process.

For the next prana exercise you need to pick a number between three and nine which has significance to you. If you are a part of the school of thought that teaches a certain number is sacred, you should use that, especially if it is connected in any way to the concept of prana. Again, find a comfortable and quiet spot and begin to breathe slowly and evenly. As you inhale, mentally count to that significant number you have chosen, hold the breath for one or two counts, and then mentally count again to that number as you exhale. Practice this process until it comes naturally whenever you are meditating.

After you are used to the basic exercise, vary the counts of the breath and note any changes you feel in your physical or mental body as you do so. By doing this you will eventually be able to chart for yourself which types of breathing put you in to certain moods, conjure up certain images or feelings, or put you in the deepest or lightest altered states. All this information can later be used to help attune yourself to your psychic goals ... Automatic Writing included!

Protecting Yourself in Meditation

Unless you are going to go deeply into a meditative state of consciousness, or plan to spend lots of time in that state doing advanced psychic work, you probably do not need elaborate physical or psychic protections. It should be enough for you to find yourself a place to work where you feel comfortable and safe from disturbances.

However, if you feel you need something more, then you should read Chapter Six which discusses this protection in detail in conjunction with the actual Automatic Writing process.

Basic Meditation

Meditation is defined in most dictionaries as being "deep in thought." While this is basically true, it is not a broad enough definition for our purposes.

Occult meditation is defined as "focused thought," or sometimes even the "absence of thought." It is a method by which only one object, symbol, word, phrase, or idea is focused upon in order to slow the cycle per second waves of the brain, inducing a sort of awakened sleep during which all facets of ourselves are in a heightened state of awareness and receptivity. In this meditative state, also referred to as an altered state of consciousness or a trance state, the subconscious and conscious minds are better connected. These two separate consciousnesses can then better communicate, not only with you and your Higher Self, but with the right and left brain hemispheres, and with other intelligences.

Achieving this state is both easy and difficult. It is easy in the sense that it has happened to you quite naturally every single day and night of your life. As you fall asleep at night you naturally slip into these lower levels of consciousness. It also happens when you read a book, watch television, or daydream. But meditation is hard in the sense that gaining conscious control over the process takes consistent practice.

Being able to achieve such a state at will is necessary to most occult practices, and occultists throughout the centuries have used various methods that have altered little over the centuries. Only the details of the visualizations used vary from tradition to tradition and from individual to individual. Some people prefer a method of using numbers to count themselves "down," others focus on a symbol relevant to their goals, some use phrases or positive affirmations, others use lavish imagery geared to induce relaxation, and others attempt to clear their minds of all thoughts.

If you already have such a method for achieving an altered state of consciousness that works well for you, you should continue to use it as your mind is already conditioned to it. If you do not have a method you like, or even if you have never practiced meditation before, you can begin to learn the process right now and start having success with it almost immediately.

First, find a place where you will not be disturbed for about thirty minutes. Voices, footsteps, and other noises you are able to filter out when you are awake can be very disturbing when you are first learning to meditate, and repeated interruptions may eventually convince your mind that relaxation is too risky. No harm will come to you if you are jolted "awake," but the sensation is most unpleasant, rather like being awakened quickly from sleep.

The first exercise you should practice is a simple one designed to help you learn to focus your consciousness. For this you will need only a simple candle. Any color or size is fine. Light the candle and get comfortable far enough away from it that staring at the flame will not hurt your eyes.

You may sit, recline or even lie down if you think you can stay awake. Just make sure the candle is clearly in view and that you don't have to crane your neck or strain yourself in any other way to look at it.

Begin to gaze at the candle flame. Don't stare; softly focus on it with partially opened eyes, blinking when you need to. Try to clear your mind of all thoughts but the candle flame. When your mind wanders—as it inevitably will in these early stages—don't worry. Just bring it back to the candle.

Practice this daily for several weeks, attempting each time to go for increasingly longer periods without having your mind wander. Start out trying for five successful minutes at a time, then work up. Make your final goal fifteen to twenty minutes of focused thought.

When you can do this exercise consistently, try to involve new dimensions of the candle in your meditation. Try focusing on a single color—such as blue—within the center of the flame. Or try to project your mind into the flame and become a part of it. This is similar to an occult practice known as astral projection, and it is another excellent way to discipline your mind.

More Advanced Meditation Techniques

The next step is to learn a basic eyes-closed meditation. Go again to that place where you will not be disturbed, assume the position you prefer, and close your eyes. You will now choose a symbol or word to focus on. If you are more attracted to sights than to sounds, choose a symbol. If you are more audio-oriented, then choose a word. Whatever you select, keep it very simple at first. Use a basic geometric form, your name or nickname, a religious symbol, or a single syllable verb or noun. Words related to occult goals such as "down," "will," "peace," "join," and "all" are frequently chosen by beginners. Squares, circles, triangles, and ovals are the easiest shapes to hold in your mind over long periods. Make these one primary color, either red, blue, or yellow.

Fix your chosen object/word in your mind and begin to see/repeat it to the exclusion of all else. Allow yourself to become totally merged with that object/symbol. Feel it, taste it, sense it. If your mind wanders, bring it back.

Again, practice this daily for several weeks, each time trying to increase your control over the process. Make your sessions twenty to thirty minutes long.

By now you should feel yourself slipping into an awakened sleep shortly after your sessions begin. This sensation tells you that you are successfully bringing down the speed of your brain waves, in other words, you have achieved controlled meditation.

If you still feel you are not doing the exercise right you might try using the countdown method. Simply close your eyes and begin slowly counting backward from any number you choose (100 is a good starting point). As you do this feel yourself falling inwards into yourself, finding the center of your being. The Buddhists teach this same practice by having the novice count their breaths as they attempt to alter their consciousness. Both methods are good and will get you to the same place. Choose the one that works best for you.

Even if you are a slow study, by now you are definitely achieving some sort of meditative state even if you may not feel you are successful, or are not as deeply into one as you would like to be. If you want something to compare your sensations to, then you might try reading a book or watching television and, when you are deeply interested in the plot, make yourself aware of the feelings you are experiencing. You will find they are similar to those you have in a light to medium altered state.

Another way to check on your progress is to look at the clock both before and after you meditate. In an altered state time becomes distorted. If you find that significantly more or less time has passed than you feel it should have, you have definitely been successful!

Brain Waves Chart

Name	Cycles/second	Condition
Beta	15-18	Normal wakefulness, alertness, study, conversational level. Person is aware of all physical sensations and bodily needs.
Alpha	8-12	Light to medium meditation, daydreaming, focused concentration, drowsiness, cat napping, some astral projection, easy guided meditations, very light sleep. Person finds waking from this level not difficult.
Theta	4-6	Deep meditation, medium to deep sleep, complex astral projection, complex guided meditation, light unconsciousness. Person finds waking from this level moderately to very difficult.
Delta	0.5-2.5	Very deep sleep, coma or deep unconsciousness. Person has little or no consciousness of physical sensations or bodily needs.

The Chakras

As mentioned before, the method of Automatic Writing outlined in this book uses the natural energy centers known as the chakras to channel down the needed power to connect you to the entities you are contacting. This chakra-link serves two basic functions: it provides a link directly from the individual doing the writing to the Collective Unconscious; and it allows the Higher Self (always conceptualized as residing in the Crown Chakra) to filter out harmful influences that may want to try to enter you during your writing. In order to be able do this you must first have:

- A basic knowledge of the chakra system, and how to balance and cleanse each chakra.

- A method by which to stimulate them.

- A method for channeling energy not your own through them.

- A method to ground the excess energy once you are finished using it.

"Chakra" is a Hindustani word roughly meaning "wheel." They are the seven spheres of concentrated energy located on the human body. These begin at the top of your head and proceed in a straight line down your body to the base of your tail bone (See illustration on opposite page).

In ancient India, where these spheres were first discovered many centuries ago, they have long been used help channel energies, heal the body and spirit, energize the body and mind, aid in prayer, and to help people to either meditate or ground themselves. Western science remained skeptical about the existence of these energy centers until recently when laboratory tests demonstrated that there were strong electromagnetic emanations coming from them.

Each chakra has its own color, number, and physical and mental signs that tell us whether it is functioning properly or not. The cleaner, clearer, and more balanced the chakra channels are the healthier we are, and—for our purposes—the easier it is for us to channel energy through them for Automatic Writing.

The first chakra is called the Root Chakra, and it is located at the base of the tail bone. It is always to be visualized as a bright red sphere slowly pulsating with energy. This is the chakra that can be called on to help ground you when you feel flighty or unable to concentrate. Some signs that it is not functioning properly are irritable bowels, spastic colon, chronic stomach upsets,

Chakras of the Human Body

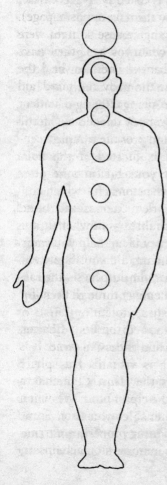

Crown (Just above the head)

Third Eye (Between and above the eyes)

Throat (Center of the hollow of the throat)

Heart Center (Middle of the breast bone)

Solar Plexus (At the center of the Solar Plexus)

Navel (Just below the navel)

Root (At the base of the tail bone)

yo-yo weight, joint pain or stiffness, the inability to concentrate, and difficulty waking up.

The second chakra is called the Navel Chakra and is located just below the navel area. It is visualized as a sphere of orange energetic light. This chakra can be activated when you feel overly emotional or need to summon extra will power. Some of the signs that it is functioning poorly are hormone imbalances, mood swings, eating disorders, sexual dysfunction, lower body infections, infertility, fungal infestations, and prostate troubles.

The third chakra is located at the Solar Plexus, the area below your breast bone often described as "the pit of the stomach," which contains an intricate network of nerves and blood vessels. When this vibrantly yellow chakra is operating at peak efficiency it can help you translate your will into action and aid you in expressing your masculine side. Some of the indications that it is blocked or weak are chronic indigestion, gastritis, ulcers, hot flashes, violent outbursts or tantrums, paranoia, blood disorders, diabetes, stress-related problems, and excessive greed.

The fourth chakra is visualized as a rich green and is known as the Heart Center. It is located at the center of the breast bone. When it is functioning properly it enables you to give and accept love and easily express your feminine side. Chronic conditions that indicate it is not working as well as it should are repeating dysfunctional relationships, allergies, heart problems, jealousy, frequent emotional outbursts, and high or low blood pressure.

Chakra number five is called the Throat Chakra and is located at the hollow in the center of the throat. It is seen as a bright true blue which throbs at the speed of sound. This chakra governs our speech and communication and can be energized to help us in our creative endeavors. Indications of a problem in the Throat Chakra are chronic sore throats or hoarseness, ringing in the ears, tonsillitis, psychosis, verbal abusiveness, Tourettes Syndrome, and such creative impediments as writer's block.

The Third Eye is perhaps the most well-known of all the chakra points. It is a sphere of rich deep indigo located between and above the eyes. Often adherents of the Hindu religion place a small blue or violet dot over the area in order to keep it energized and open. Psychics and other New Age people often tap into the force of this chakra to aid them in numerous psychic endeavors as it governs the ability to see both the inner and outer planes of being. Some signs that it is blocked or not working properly are persistent vision problems, sleep disorders, snoring, nightmares, migraines, dental problems, and many types of poltergeist activity.

The last chakra is the Crown Chakra located just above the head. This center is always visualized as a vivid violet sphere pulsating faster than the speed of light. It is often conceptualized as the place where the Higher Self resides and, as an energy center, is a tool for spiritual growth and a link for connecting ourselves with other intelligences. The energy of this chakra is used both consciously and unconsciously in psychic work, and when involved in study, astral projection, meditation, and creative dreaming. Indications of a serious problem with the chakra include dogmatism, smugness, depression, forgetfulness, loneliness, chemical imbalances, Parkinson's Disease, learning disorders, severe neurological disorders, memory loss, and most cancers.

This list of chakra dysfunctions is not intended to take the place of a doctor in self-diagnosis, but instead to point out how potent these seven spheres of energy are and to suggest which ones might need cleansing or opening in order to help in healing.

Chakra Balancing/Cleansing Exercise

Before you can channel energy through the chakras for Automatic Writing, you first must learn to visualize and energize them. Energizing them is another word for opening them so that energy can flow freely through them. Later this will be the method by which you bring down the channeled energy of the collective unconscious into your writing arm. While you learn to do this you can also learn to cleanse and balance them so they operate at peak efficiency.

There are numerous ways to cleanse and balance the chakras, and nearly all of them involve visualization while trying to sense, or psychically "see," their physical condition, then, if need be, eliminating any disease from them.

To perform this exercise you will need thirty to forty minutes in a quiet, undisturbed working space, and a hard surface where you can sit upright, keeping your spine as straight as possible. Doing this places the chakras in a straight line up and down your body and enables them to more efficiently channel energy. For instance, think of the chakras in your body as a garden hose. If the hose has kinks and twists in it, the water will not flow freely and fully. But straighten it out and open the tube inside to its maximum potential, and you have a clear, unimpeded flow of water.

Some people like to practice this exercise while sitting on the floor in the eastern Lotus position (both feet on the inner-knee area and hands on the thighs with palms opened and upward), and others—probably the majority of Westerners—prefer a hard-backed chair. Kitchen chairs, settles, or deacon's benches are excellent choices.

If you are using a chair, slide back in it as far as you can, center yourself on it, and place your feet flat on the floor in front of you. Your knees do not have to be together. Let them fall apart slightly if that is what is comfortable to you. Physical tenseness or strain of any kind can inhibit the energy flow are you trying to create. Rest your hands on your legs in any position that feels right. People who follow the Oriental teachings like to hold their palms upward, and those who follow the Indian traditions like to adopt a Mudra position in which the thumb and forefinger are held together. Do what feels most comfortable.

If you are sitting on the floor in a Lotus position make sure your spine is straight before you begin.

Start by taking a few deep breaths and allow your eyes to fall lightly closed. Continue breathing deeply and, with each exhale, feel yourself relaxing more.

Now begin to actively place yourself in a light meditative state. You may use the methods explained above or use one of your own. As long as your brain waves are slowed and your body is fully relaxed you can do this exercise.

When you feel you are in a light altered state of consciousness (deeper is fine, but not necessary at this point), visualize the all-knowing energy of the creative power of the universe high above you. Some people like to imagine that this is the life-giving energy of a benevolent deity. Make sure you can really see and feel this. Practice until you do because, later, we will bring down a similar energy from the collective unconscious in order to do our Automatic Writing. See this creative power as a stream of pure light energy. If you need to visualize this energy as a color in order to see it clearly, make it white, gold, silver, or electric blue. See this energy pulsating with all the power of the ages, and feel it come down like a tall waterfall and enter your body through the Crown Chakra.

Allow the energy to mingle for a moment or two with the Crown area and let your Higher Self get used to its presence, to help alert it that you are going to be consciously calling upon its services soon.

Visualize the Crown Chakra as a vivid violet sphere being expanded, enhanced, and bought into perfect balance by the creative energy. Try to sense or "see" any dark spots in the chakra or any areas of the sphere that are not pulsating at the same rate as the rest of the sphere. If you have had practice reading auras, this should be an easy task to master. These dark spots indicate a blockage or a possible disease within the energy field, and cleaning it now could prevent an illness later. Allow the creative energy to consume the dark spots and destroy them by replacing them with a clear, pure colored light which is perfectly healthy and strong.

When you feel you have fully opened, balanced, and cleaned your Crown Chakra, allow the energy to move down to your Third Eye and repeat the process. Make sure you restore it to a rich indigo with no dark spots or uneven pulsations.

As you work this exercise from the Crown down, each chakra will vibrate at a slower and lower rate. Look to the "Chakra Quick Reference Chart" on Page 128 at the numbers column to get an idea of how much more intense the vibrational rate of each should be in comparison to the one before. Use these to help you understand the subtle energies of the various chakra points.

Continue down through each energy center focusing especially on any chakra which may effect illnesses or problems you have. Pay particular attention to restoring the vivid color and throbbing sensation to each one.

Move the energy into the Throat Chakra, then down to the Heart Center. Pay particular attention to the Solar Plexus which tends to be a problem for most of us because it is related to stress disorders and we live in a stress-filled world. When you finish the Solar Plexus move down to the Navel and then to the Root Chakra.

The Root Chakra is the slowest moving and will often seem to have a sluggish sort of throbbing. For this reason it was assigned low numbers by the mystics who sought to discover its magickal correspondences. Don't try to speed it up; this is its natural state. Merely cleanse and balance it, making sure that all parts of it are pulsating in unison.

If you have trouble remembering what the colors of each are, just remember the order of the colors of a rainbow. From top to bottom, here are the respective chakra colors:

> Crown—Violet
> Third Eye—Indigo
> Throat—Blue
> Heart Center—Green
> Solar Plexus—Yellow
> Navel—Orange
> Root—Red

When you have finished cleansing and balancing the Root Chakra, spend a few minutes allowing yourself the pleasure of feeling the freshly released energy flowing through your body and knowing that it is restoring you to perfect mental, physical, and spiritual balance. Capture the feeling of this power streaming through you so you can easily recognize it when you do your Automatic Writing.

Chakra Quick

Chakra	Location	Color(s)	Governs/Associations
Root	Base of the Tail Bone	Red	Health, intestines, sexuality Earth Element, centering, individuality, snakes, stability, personal security, sense of smell, cattle, lead, Saturn, the Earth, evergreen trees, the Square
Navel	Just Below the Navel	Orange	Desire, willpower, feminine power, blood, emotions, Water Element, sea herbs and stones, sea animals, grief and joy, reproductive organs, the Circle, Neptune
Solar Plexus	Center of the Solar Plexus	Yellow	Digestion, masculine power, Fire Element, goats, heat, anger, topaz, carnelian
Heart Center	Center of the Breast Bone	Green	Love, emotions, memory, birds, Air Element, lavender, compassion, heart and lungs, the Moon
Throat	Center of the Hollow of Throat	Blue White	Speech, communication, music, hearing, writing, creativity, the Triangle, Mercury, thyroid, mouth, elephants and lions
Third Eye	Between and just above the Eyes	Indigo Silver	Psychicism, the Oval, sight, light, perception, the winged Deities, quartz, the Mental Body
Crown	Just above the Head	Violet Silver Gold	Higher Self, Spirit Element, the brain, thought, all time, diamond, the Lotus, full moon, spirituality, the Astral Body, nervous system

Reference Chart

Numbers Chronic Signs of Chakra Energy Blockage

Numbers	Chronic Signs of Chakra Energy Blockage
1, 3	Irritable bowels, spastic colon, constipation, diarrhea, weight swings, arthritis, inability to concentrate
2, 7	Hormone imbalances, mood swings, eating disorders, sexual dysfunction, urinary tract infections, vaginal infections, prostate disorders
3, 10, 33	Indigestion, hot flashes, violent temper, tantrums, paranoia, blood disorders, sugar intolerance, diabetes, excessive greed
4, 12, 99	Dysfunctional relationships, heart arrhythmia, anxiety attacks, allergies, respiratory problems, high or low blood pressure, most heart conditions
5, 16, 100	Sore throat, hoarseness, ringing in the ears, tonsillitis, psychosis, verbal abusiveness, Tourettes syndrome
6, 700	Vision problems, sleep disorders, nightmares, migraines, dental problems, some psychic disturbances, human-caused poltergeist activity
7, 9, 1000	Closed-mindedness, dogmatism, depression, forgetfulness, loneliness, chemical imbalances, Parkinson's Disease, most cancers, severe neurological disorders, memory loss

Before you end this exercise you should close or partially close any chakra you feel does not need to be left wide open. For instance, if you often allow yourself to be easily hurt by people you may not want to keep your Heart Center wide open. Close it down a bit before you quit to minimize your chances of being hurt. To do this, simply visualize the chakra contracting and decreasing the intensity of its color but not pulsating less strongly. You only want to shut it down enough to leave it less vulnerable, while still allowing your body's energies to continue to flow through it.

In order to quit this exercise you should visualize the creative energy flow ceasing. Then visualize all the chakras together turning a vivid, clean white. White is often used at the end of color therapy sessions to help stabilize the treatment, and it is a technique which works well in this exercise, too.

You have two choices as to where you send the excess energy inside you that was not able to be absorbed by the chakras: you can send it into the ground, or return it to its source. This idea of grounding or returning unused energy is an ancient and respected occult practice. By leaving excess energy inside, you can upset your system as easily as by having too little energy and, if it finds its way out of you on its own, it can cause minor psychic disturbances. Where you decide to send it depends on how you are feeling at the time. If you feel you need to focus more on higher matters such as spirituality, compassion, etc., then you should opt to send the energy upwards towards its source. This helps keep you focused on those higher goals after the exercise is finished. On the other hand, if you feel flighty, unfocused, or unable to concentrate, you should ground the energy, thereby providing you with a psychic link to the stabilizing force of Mother Earth.

Begin to feel the excess energy moving toward either your Root or Crown Chakra depending on which direction you have decided to send it. When you feel it has all been gathered there you should do one of the following.

• To Send The Energy Up:

Visualize it flying straight up from your head in a stream of pale blue white. Remain with it until it disappears in the heavens so high you cannot follow it with your mental eyes any longer. Sense that it has been reabsorbed by the creative power you drew it from or, if you prefer, by a benevolent deity.

• To Send The Energy Down:

If you are seated in a chair, with your eyes still closed, slowly stand and visualize it streaming straight down between your feet rather like something that would roll off your lap as you stand. If you are in a Lotus position, feel the energy pass straight out of your Root Chakra and into the ground beneath you. In either case, mentally see it being absorbed deep into the body of Mother Earth and feel yourself being connected with that stabilizing influence.

Whether you are now sitting or standing, stop and take a few moments to re-orient yourself to your normal consciousness. Feel yourself coming up from your trance level and your mind gearing up for life in your normal waking reality. Allow yourself to remember where you are and what you are doing, and to consciously feel the sensations of physical life returning to your body. When you feel you have accomplished this you may open your eyes and go about your business.

If you practice cleansing and balancing your chakras on a regular basis you will, in time, notice definite benefits. You will feel more balanced and focused, you will be healthier, better able to concentrate, and all your psychic endeavors—including your ultimate goal of Automatic Writing—will be much more successful.

Steps in the Chakra Cleansing/Balancing Exercise

1. Sit with your spine as straight as possible.
2. Allow your eyes to close.
3. Breathe deeply and relax.
4. Achieve a light meditative state.
5. Bring down the creative energy.
6. Energize the Chakras one by one.
7. Feel each one open.
8. Sense or "see" any dark spots.
9. Cleanse each chakra.
10. Focus most strongly on those relating to any illnesses.
11. Flood each chakra with fresh energy and color.
12. Visualize them all working at peak efficiency.
13. Close or partially close any chakras you need to close.
14. Ground or return unused energy as desired.
15. Spend a moment re-orienting your consciousness.
16. Open your eyes.

Purging...For Beginners

If this will be your first attempt ever at Automatic Writing your mind is no doubt cluttered with a myriad of unformed, but still present, pre-conceived ideas, hopes, and fears regarding the messages you might receive. Before you move on and actually begin Automatic Writing, the best thing you can do for yourself is to have a fantasy practice session to purge from your psyche all expectations and/or terrors that may make your efforts more difficult in the long run.

To purge your psyche of these detrimental influences, simply take a piece of paper and a pen and sit down and begin to write. You will not, and should not, be in an altered state. Think about what you wish to say to yourself and then allow your imagination to run wild. Write down those things you would want to see written to you in your fondest dreams or what you would dread reading in your worst nightmare. Tell yourself that you are guilty or not guilty for some past misdeed. Make peace with your late grandfather. Create a communication from your greatest hero or heroine either past or present. Tell yourself that you are about to meet the love of your life. Say whatever feels good and right to you.

Yes, you will be making it all up. But in this case fantasy has its purpose. By allowing yourself to give vent to these preconceived notions that might later try to manifest in, or interfere with, your writing, you will bring them from your sub-conscious into your consciousness. You will see them on paper before you, an act which will purge much of their power over you. If it is a hope, you can read it and then feel the thrill of it. If it is a terror, you can see how little there really is to fear from a few words scribbled on a piece of paper. And, if at a later time, any of these ideas do appear in your writing you will be in a better position to analyze and use the information since you have already taken this time to deal with it.

Don't scrimp on this step. The fantasy writ-ing process takes less than thirty minutes and can be very illuminating and cathartic.

Opening Your Psychic Channels With the Chakras

Once you learn to channel energy through the chakras at will, you can easily use them to chan-nel the energy and/or entities you need for your Automatic Writing. In fact, tapping into this flow of all-knowing energy can aid you in any type of divination you choose.

In the next chapter, as we go step by step through the actual Automatic Writing process, you will learn to channel the omniscient power of the Collective Unconscious in order to contact any intelligence you wish.

Make That Commitment of 60 Days

You are now ready to attempt actual Automatic Writing. If you have learned to channel energy through your chakras you should have no difficulty learning this art fairly quickly. However, if you do have trouble, realize that it, like any worthwhile endeavor, takes practice and persistence. As mentioned earlier, you should promise to give yourself a full sixty days during which you will practice your writing each and every day. At the end of this time virtually everyone should be able to use the oracle of Automatic Writing.

If, at the end of sixty days, you still are unsuccessful, take a week or two off and then try again. Sometimes allowing yourself time to think about a project, or time to clear up other mental clutter, can make all the difference.

Make this old adage your personal motto: "Anything worth having is worth working for."

❧ 6 ❧

Doing It!
(In 15 Easy Steps)

As with any occult practice, your preparatory rituals for Automatic Writing become very important because they help condition the mind to the idea that profound change is about to take place, making it easier to ultimately find success. This is similar to the way you would train a dog in that you use an identical training routine repeatedly until the animal—in this case, your mind—gets the idea, then, like the dog, it happily obeys your every command, glad to please you.

To begin, read through this chapter and get a full understanding of what you will be doing, then memorize each of the fifteen basic steps so that you can perform your Automatic Writing exercises smoothly and confidently. Taking the time now to do this will greatly aid in your eventual success. Nothing will be more detrimental to your progress than having to stop each step of the way to check with a written text to see if you are on line.

Step 1: Gather Your Equipment

This seems like a logical place to start, but many beginners often pick equipment that can hamper their progress.

You should always choose a pen to work with rather than a pencil, which requires more pressure in order to be legible. The best pens to use are those with felt tips or padded roller balls; they enable the pen to glide smoothly over the surface of the paper. The less effort you have to put into making the pen write, the easier it will be for your Higher Self to make it work for you.

Whether you choose plain or ruled paper is immaterial, though most people like having the lines to keep their words flowing straight because it makes them easier to read. In either case, use regular sized notebook paper. The standard 8-1/2 x 11 inch school paper is a perfect choice, and is both inexpensive and easy to find. Do not choose steno pads, or other pages of smaller-sized paper. It is difficult to turn pages in the middle of an automatic communication, even for the advanced practitioner. Therefore, you want as large a surface to write on as is practical.

It is better still to use only one sheet at a time. Stacking paper, as in a spiral-bound notebook, can sometimes make it harder to write on because of the added thickness and it can frustrate beginning efforts.

Plan to have a solid backing to your paper. Most people practice Automatic Writing while sitting up and balancing the paper on their laps, while some (myself included) prefer a table or desk. If you use your lap and don't want the bulk of an entire stack of paper slowing your pen, you might place a piece of heavy cardboard, a kitchen cutting board, a clipboard, an over-sized hardback book or lap-top desk underneath to make your writing surface more sturdy. The work surface should also be large enough for you to rest your forearm on easily without having it sliding off.

Unless you prefer to write in the Lotus position (explained in Chapter Five), the chair you choose should be similar to the one you use for cleaning your chakras. It should be hard, sturdy, and enable you to sit erect, but comfortably, with your spine as straight as possible.

If you will be attempting to contact a deceased person during your writing, it will be helpful to wear one of their personal items. A piece of jewelry they always wore is best, but any small item will do to help you forge the bond you need to make contact.

Other "equipment" you may wish to have could consist of candles, talismans, stones, amulets, etc., all of which we will explore further.

Step 2: Go to Your Work Place

Your work place can be anywhere you have peace, quiet, and privacy for as long as it takes to finish the task at hand. Sessions usually run no longer than ten to twenty minutes including preparation time, but some, especially as you are learning, may run considerably longer.

It is best to choose a place that you do not associate with excessive mental stimulation or activity. This rules out libraries, computer rooms, game rooms, and most family rooms. The residual vibrations from these active things can distract you even when they are not in use. Your kitchen or dining room, formal living room, bedroom, or even your bathroom are all excellent choices.

Don't laugh at the idea of using the bathroom to practice Automatic Writing. It may actually be your best choice in the house. It is a room where one is almost always assured of having complete privacy, it is associated with relaxation, and it is usually so small that many of the distractions inherent in other rooms of the house are automatically eliminated. In most apartments and in many homes the bathroom often has no outside windows, which helps filter away outside noises such as the neighbor's kids playing, or barking dogs. In the bathroom you also have a built-in seat which, with the lid closed, might just be the perfect chair for keeping your spine straight.

You also don't want glaring lights in the room you use. They can be a big distraction, especially when you open your eyes to write and have to readjust your vision. Keep the lighting soft and warm.

Wherever you choose to work, try to be consistent in using the same place until you are proficient at your art. Again, this is part of conditioning your mind to your goal.

Step 3: Clear Your Work Area

This is the step where you truly begin ritually preparing yourself to practice Automatic Writing.

You will need to clear your work area of all clutter, both the physical and the psychic. To clear the physical clutter simply pick up and put away all the things that may distract you. If your son's baseball cards are within eyesight they can be great detractors with their multi-colors and their strong association with physical action. If you are a neat freak like me, they may also make you feel guilty for not stopping to put them where they belong, and this idea will nag at you until you get up and do it.

You needn't make your work area spartan. Merely sit down ahead of time in the place where you will be working and try to see what things might catch your eye and later break your concentration. In the softly focused state you will be seeing with, normally inoffensive decor can distract you.

Next you will need to clear the area of emotional influences and psychic clutter, which include such normally unfelt things as negative vibrations, residual energies, and other things that practiced occultists have long known are not conducive to their work. How you choose to eliminate them will depend largely on your background, religion, and past experiences.

For example, if you are Catholic, the sprinkling of Holy Water around the area might best banish the unwanted energies. If you practice Ceremonial Magick you may want to do a Rose Cross or Lesser Banishing Ritual. Followers of Eastern religions might employ the ringing of ritual bells which has long been known to be effective in cleaning out occult work areas. Salt water also has clearing abilities, as do many incenses. Try the incense of cinnamon, frankincense, or sandalwood.

The important thing is to do what makes you feel the area you are going to work in is free of outside, unwanted, and distracting influences.

If you are going to use a table or desk rather than your lap, make sure to cleanse it too, preferably with salt water. If you would rather not use water try another small banishing ritual. For example, trace a protective symbol on its surface or mentally see the unwanted energy flowing from it harmlessly into the ground. Your visualization is the key to doing it right!

Using your imagination and creativity to psychically clear your work space can set up powerful subliminal triggers in your mind that a profound change in consciousness is about to take place, especially if the ritual(s) you create for yourself is used consistently and repeatedly. The following is a sample Clearing Ritual designed to banish negative vibrations from an area. Feel free to use or adapt it to your own needs and ideas.

Clearing Ritual

For this ritual you will need incense in a portable form (i.e.; a joss stick or loose in a censer), a white candle, matches, and the pure power of your visualization abilities.

Make sure you have all the needed items with you before you begin. Step into the center of the area you will work in, or as near to the center as it is possible to be, and stand facing any direction you choose to state aloud your intent.

> *I stand here, in the center of the*
> *universe, fearlessly prepared to contact*
> *other intelligences. Only the*
> *benevolent, loving, higher entities who*
> *love me and wish me success are invited into*

> *this space. No negative powers,*
> *influences, energies, or entities are*
> *welcome here in this sacred space.*
> *Bane Be Gone!*

Hold the incense in front of you while walking slowly in a counter-clockwise circle surrounding your work area. See the smoke filling the space around you, feel its high, pure vibrations driving away all lower entities and energies that may be hovering around. Traveling once around the circle is usually enough, but if you have a number that you or a tradition you belong to holds as sacred, you can circle around that many times instead.

When you are back to your starting point, put the incense down. Now take up the candle and hold it in front of you, saying:

> *May this candle of white* (or state
> the color you have chosen to use),
> *whose pure and sacred flame guards*
> *and enfolds me like the arms of a*
> *warm and loving mother, continue to*
> *burn away all negative influences*
> *which seek to enter here.*

Light the candle and focus softly on its golden flame for a few moments, feeling its power and seeing it doing its job for you.

If you like, you may walk with the candle around the circle as you did with the incense. When you are finished, put the candle down.

When you feel your area is free from negativity you should make a statement to indicate that the ritual is finished. Words or phrases such as "It is done," "So mote it be," or "Amen," are all appropriate.

After this you can begin your Automatic Writing when ready. You may leave the candle burning throughout the entire process if you like.

Step 4: Protect Yourself

While the risks taken in Automatic Writing are negligible, you still do not want just anything or anyone coming into you and leaving messages. You want to avoid contact with lower entities, mischievous spirits, angry discarnates, or elementals, and discourage them from playing games with you or leaving unsettling messages. The method of facilitating Automatic Writing we are using, which allows the energy to come through the Crown Chakra, enables the Higher Self to filter out most of these negative influences, but, just the same, you should not take unnecessary chances.

There are almost as many methods of psychic protection as there are people on the planet.

Adept occultists have long taught us that this protective power is really in our own minds, so the most effective method of protection is what most strongly symbolizes a protective force to you.

Because I follow one of the many earth religions, I like to cast a circle of protective energy about me. This is done either with my forefinger, mind, or a ritual tool. I simply project out my will to have a protective circle about me, allowing it to manifest through one of these objects as I physically "draw" it while traveling in a clockwise, or deosil, motion. If you would like to use a circle for protection, you should first decide how you want to "draw" it, then, as you do, simply visualize it as a vibrant blue-white barrier of energy rising around you through which no unwanted force can pass. Always remember to draw it clockwise as this is the direction traditionally associated with increase, gain, and constructivity.

After my circle is cast I call upon my deities, and other friendly entities, to further watch over me during my efforts. Certainly asking for divine protection is nearly as old as humankind, but it will work best for those who truly believe in the power and goodwill of their Gods and Goddesses. If you have any doubts, find another method of protection.

Some people unfamiliar with the uses of a circle will ask why it is to be visualized as a bright blue-white. The answer is simply that this is its color. For centuries, those with the psychic sensitivity to actually see the circle say that this is how it appears.

Another common method of protection among New Age people is the deliberate strengthening of the aura. The aura is the energy field that surrounds all living things. Generally it remains invisible to the naked eye but, with a little effort, one can train themselves to see it. By mentally reinforcing the thickness of the aura and then mentally projecting it outwards from the body you can create a protective barrier around yourself which resembles a large egg or cocoon. If you like, you can add color to the auric field such as white or gold, the traditional colors of protection.

Another method of protection, and a very ancient one, is to employ a natural protective device known as an amulet. Amulets are things that are found in nature which symbolize protection to their bearers. Such items include stones and crystals, flowers, feathers, plants, twigs, and fossils. They are easy to use because they are believed to be empowered by the natural forces of the earth, and require no added energy from their bearers.

Stones are probably the most popular amulets because they are easily portable, keep forever, and can be found in abundance. Some

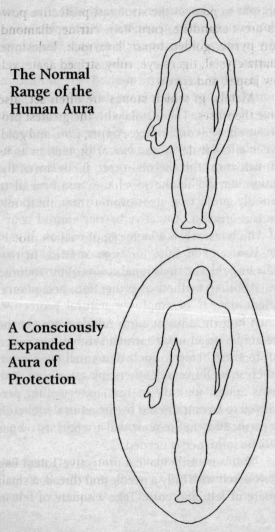

**The Normal
Range of the
Human Aura**

**A Consciously
Expanded
Aura of
Protection**

thought to possess the strongest protective powers are alexandrite, carnelian, citrine, diamond, iron pyrite, golden topaz, lava rock, lodestone, quartz crystal, tiger's eye, ruby, striped agate, yellow jasper, and zircon.

Metals, in which stones are often set, also have their uses. The metals with the greatest protective energies are bronze, copper, iron, and gold. Silver offers little in the way of protection as its affinities are with the inner-self, the realm of the dream world and the psychic, a good metal to have as an aid to divination, but not one to rely on to guard you.

Talismans can also be employed as protective devices. These differ from amulets in that they are created and empowered (by focused visualization) by the user rather than being found in nature.

From the ancient earth religions we get the protective pouch-style talisman sometimes called a Totem Bag. This consists of a small hand-sewn pouch in which protective items are placed. The bag is infused with the will and energy of the person who makes it, then it is carried in a pocket or worn around the neck or waist when its owner feels its influence is needed.

You can easily make a protective Totem Bag for yourself with only a needle and thread, a small square of felt, and cord. Take a square of felt in any color you feel represents protection. Again, white and gold are the traditional colors, but this shouldn't limit you. If you follow Women's Spirituality you might want to use silver for the Goddess, or if you have an affinity for the old Roman gods you might want to choose red, the color of that celestial fighter Mars. How big you will want to make the bag depends largely on what you intend to put into it, but a finished bag will be about two by two inches square, big enough to hold almost anything you want to put into it and still small enough to wear or carry.

Cut your felt into a piece 4½ inches long by 2½ inches across. Next, fold the piece in half so that you have a square. Sew up the two sides that border against the fold, leaving a hem about a half-inch wide. As you sew, be sure to strongly visualize the job of protection that you want the finished talisman to perform for you. Put as much of your desire and will into it as possible.

When you have finished sewing up the two sides, turn your little pouch inside out so that the sewn seams are on the inside of the pocket. Next, gather the items you wish to put inside. These can be anything that signals protection to you. Add stones, herbs, jewelry, nail clippings, hair, icons— whatever fits easily inside. Be sure that you don't stuff the bag to the point that its weight and bulk will become a distraction when you do your Automatic Writing.

Making a Totem Bag

Step 1: Fold the felt in half and stitch up the two open sides along the dotted lines.

Step 2: Turn the bag inside out, place desired items inside, then stitch up the top opening along the dotted lines.

Step 3: Attach a cord, string, or thin rope to the corners if desired to wear the bag around your neck or waist.

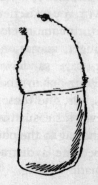

When your Totem Bag has been filled with all its needed objects, sew the top shut, again remembering to visualize your need as you work.

Next, take your cord, rope, or string, and measure it against the part of your body you wish to wear it on—usually your waist or neck—and cut off that amount. Sew the ends securely to the corners of the bag so that you can wear it without fear of losing it.

Familiar prayers or rituals are also good sources of protection. For instance, people who practice Ceremonial Magick might wish to employ their Lesser Banishing Ritual as a means of protection, Catholics may wish to cross themselves, Protestants might choose to pray the Lord's Prayer, and Jews might want to recite the Shema. In addition to using a circle, Pagans may choose to ring ritual bells or spread protective herbs around their work area. Many of these herbs are common, and you probably already have some of them in your kitchen. They include basil, bay, chives, cinnamon, cloves, dill, frankincense, garlic, ginger, marjoram, nutmeg, onion, oregano, parsley, sage, sandalwood, and thyme.

Religious symbols are potent talismans for most of us, and these can be employed in one of three ways: they can be worn, as in a piece of jewelry; placed in a pocket; or drawn with your pen on the top of your writing paper. You can also have the object near you, either sitting on the table or desk top or placed near your work chair.

These protective religious icons are diverse. They include, but are not limited to, the Latin Cross (Christian), the Star of David (Jewish), the Ankh (Egyptian), the Hand of God (Spanish/Sephardic), the All-Seeing Eye (Middle Eastern), the Rose Cross (Various Paths), the Horn of Isis (Egyptian), Sun Symbols (Native American), Kachina Dolls (Navajo), the Bible (Judeo-Christian), the Koran (Islamic), representations of Buddha (Buddhist), and/or other religious statuary from the various world religions. The only thing you must remember is to make sure that the item you use will not in any way distract your thoughts or pull your eye away from the task at hand.

I once knew someone who felt that if a holy book was used as a lap-top writing desk underneath him as he wrote, providing a strong and positive foundation, that no harmful or negative messages could come into his Automatic Writing. While various negative actions and ideas have at some time been attached to nearly all sacred writings, it can't be over-emphasized that protection comes down to what you and no one else, believe will work. Below are a list of common holy books from the major world religions. If one of these appeals to you as a source of divine protection

Latin cross
This is the symbol of the Christian religion and has been used to invoke protection for about 1500 years.

Rose Cross or Equal-Armed Cross
This ancient symbol is a cross that sits upright and whose arms are of equal length. As a protective device it had been used in occult rituals since antiquity.

Star of David
This symbol of the Jewish religion is also one of the earliest known symbols of the Creator. The double triangle also represents all four of the alchemical elements united in manifestation.

Pentagram
This is another ancient glyph that is the accepted symbol of Western paganism. With apex up, it represents many things, including protection.

The All-Seeing Eye
This symbol is so old that no scholar has dared to take a stand on exactly where it came from, though the general consensus is that it originated in the Middle East. The rays represent the glory of the Creator; the triangle, the manifestation of creation; and the eye is the omniscient eye of the Creative Deity.

Horn of Isis
This symbol comes from ancient Egypt where it is associated with the Goddess Isis. Its crescent shape links it to the moon and to psychic awakening. Many wear it today as a protective amulet.

and/or inspiration, then it is certainly worth experimenting with.

Sacred Writing	Religion
Agamas	Jainism
Analects	Confucianism
Apocrypha	Roman Catholicism
Avestas	Zoroastrianism
Bhagavad Gita	Hinduism
Bible	Judeo-Christian
Book of the Dead	Egyptian Paganism
Book of the Dead	Lamaism
Book of Lights	Paganism
Book of Mormon	Mormon Christianity
Book of Shadows	Paganism
Buddhist Canons	Lamaism
I Ching	Taoism
Kethuvim-Nevi'im	Judaism
Key(s) of Solomon	Hermetic Magick
K'Ing Ching	Confucianism
Koji Ki	Shinto
Koran	Islam
New Testament	Christianity
Nihongi	Shinto
Tao Te'Ching	Taoism
Torah	Judaism
Tripitakas	Buddhism
Upanishads	Hinduism
Vedas	Hinduism
Yengishiki	Shinto

I cannot emphasize enough that you should use what feels right to you, because only that will give you the confidence and peace of mind you need to be successful in your Automatic Writing. After all, fear is the greatest stumbling block that exists, and that holds true for any effort you undertake.

Step 5: Write Out Your Question

After you have completed the first four steps, it will be time to get comfortable in the spot where you will work. Sit down, and begin to feel yourself relaxing, focusing on what you are about to do. It is important not only that you sit as straight as possible to facilitate the energy flow, but also, unless you are using a Lotus position, that you place both feet flat on the floor in front of you. Avoid the temptation to cross your legs or ankles either for comfort or to give yourself a better lap desk. Crossing your legs will only set up tensions in your body that can distract you later on and, as you will spend approximately twenty to thirty minutes in this position, your circulation will slow, making you very uncomfortable before you are finished. Attempting to adjust position midway through your efforts can also break your concentration and further hamper your chances of success.

After you are seated and have your paper in front of you and your pen in your writing hand, at the top of your paper, in as clear and precise terms as you can manage, write out the question or issue you wish to receive commentary on. Try not to make it too lengthy, but be sure you say all that needs to be said. This clarifies in your mind exactly what you are dealing with before you start involving other entities in your problem, and it also alerts your Higher Self to the issue at hand.

If you don't have a burning issue or problem to be dealt with at this time, simply ask for a helpful or encouraging message from your Spirit Guide or Higher Self. Often this type of open-ended communication yields the best results.

If you are seeking your answers from an entity other than your Higher Self, address that being in your question, much as you would if you were writing them a letter. For example, you might write, "Grandmother Mitchell, should I consider marrying David or not?"

If you are planning to receive your answers from your Higher Self (sometimes called getting your answers from "within") then you need not address yourself formally. Just clearly write out the question or issue.

Step 6: Place Yourself in a Meditative State

Following your own method, or any of the ones outlined in the previous chapter, place yourself in a medium-level meditative state. If you cannot get down this far, don't worry. Do the best you can for now and keep practicing until you can go fairly deep at will. The best thing for you to do at this point is to close your eyes, breathe deeply, and concentrate on what you wish to accomplish. If you can relax and focus enough to do this, the rest will come to you in time with practice.

Step 7: Bring Energy Into Your Chakras

Following the guidelines in the "Chakra Cleansing/Balancing Exercise" from the previous chapter, begin to draw energy into yourself. But, this time, instead of drawing down the energy from a creative power or deity, draw it down from the omniscient source we normally call the Collective Unconscious. This mass of psychic energy, also known in some circles as the Akashic Records, is believed to contain all the knowledge and experience which ever was and ever will be. It is the source of all our answers when we use any divinatory device. If you wish to visualize it in order to more easily draw from it, you should picture it as a huge, nebulous, cloud-like mass of whitish energy floating high above the universe.

The Collective Unconscious contains all the bad as well as the good influences we wish to understand, but you should remember that, because we are filtering it through the Crown Chakra, the Higher Self, always your ally and protector, will be on guard to help filter out any uninvited entities which seek to intrude.

Those of you who are familiar with the writings and work of psychic Edgar Cayce or psychologist Carl Jung are already familiar with the concept of the Collective Unconscious, and are probably comfortable with it. Those of you who are not may wish to seek out the many books written by and about these popular and influential figures. Whether or not you agree with all their concepts, they produced intriguing and ground-breaking discoveries into the human psyche that bear consideration.

Below are outlined each of the steps for drawing down this energy. If you need to review the chakras and their related colors in detail please refer to the "Chakra Cleansing/Balancing Exercise" in Chapter Five.

Sometimes my Automatic Writing students will ask why they need to draw energy into all

Visualizing the Collective Unconscious

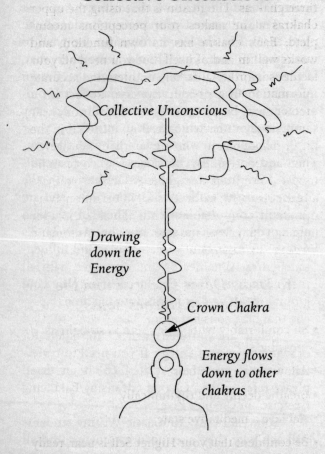

Collective Unconscious

Drawing
down the
Energy

Crown Chakra

Energy flows
down to other
chakras

their chakras, and not just the ones above the writing arm, particularly since most psychic work teaches you to focus solely on the upper two or three chakras. The reason is that using the upper chakras alone makes your perceptions incomplete. Each chakra has its own function, and works well in and of itself, but you need all your faculties in order to gather complete and accurate information in a psychic exercise. Reflect for a moment on how many times a day you hear someone say, "I had a gut feeling," "I felt it in the pit of my stomach," or "I knew it in my heart." The intestines, stomach and heart all correspond to the lower chakras through which you are already receiving extra-sensory information every minute of every day. They are valuable tools for helping you receive and interpret your Automatic Writing—use them!

To Draw Down Energy From the Collective Unconscious

- Sit comfortably with your spine as straight as possible.

- Allow your eyes to close.

- Breathe deeply and rhythmically.

- Achieve a meditative state.

- Be confident that your Higher Self is near, ready to protect you from unwanted entities and energies.

- Visualize the Collective Unconscious floating high in the heavens above you—feel its immensity and power.

- Bring down the energy of the Collective Unconscious into your Crown Chakra, see it as a beam of pure energy connecting to you.

- By moving the beam down your body, energize the chakras one by one starting with the Crown and ending at the Root.

- Feel yourself filling with intense psychic power.

- Visualize, or sense, the entity or energy with whom you wish to communicate.

- Feel that specific energy flowing into you from the Collective Unconscious, coming down to your Higher Self, ready to come into your conscious mind.

Step 8: Focus on Your Question

This step seems like common sense, but you would be surprised how many beginners are more interested in thinking about other things as they sit down to work. If this is your first time trying Automatic Writing, you will find that you are thinking about the position of your hand, the chair you're in, or anxiously anticipating what the experience is going to be like. This is, unfortunately, quite natural, and you will have to fight the tendency.

As difficult as it may be to focus, do not let your mind dwell on your anticipated outcome; this could affect the reliability of your answers. Think about the question or issue at hand, without forming preconceived ideas about it. Save that for after you have your written commentary in front of you and can analyze it with a clear head.

If you are planning to contact an entity other than your own Higher Self, you should also visualize that being answering your question.

Step 9: Bring The Energy Into Your Writing Arm

Your writing arm should rest loosely over your paper with your pen in hand. Be sure to hold your arm with the least amount of tension needed to still grasp the pen.

You should concentrate on your question or issue, having already drawn the needed energy down through your chakras. Now you must allow the excess energy flowing through you to flow into your writing arm and down into your hand. Think of this energy flow as if it were part of a long telephone wire leading from the Collective Unconscious to your waiting hand.

If you are contacting someone other than your Higher Self, sense his/her energy filling you, or sense it pouring into your Higher Self at the

Crown Chakra where it will be screened for safety before being given to you. You should still be thinking of your question as well as sensing who will be answering it.

To get the collected energy flowing directly into your writing arm, focus on concentrating the excess power into the center of your body. Have it flow into your Heart Center and see it glow a bright green-white as the surge of power floods into it. Feel the power growing in intensity and sense your intimate connection with the source of all knowledge.

Allow that energy to flow gently into your writing arm. Visualize it moving on down and feel it as it goes. Some people say they actually experience a tingling sensation at this point either in their hands, their Heart Chakra, or on the top of their heads. Don't let this bother you—it is perfectly natural, and it is further proof that the psychic energy you are channeling is indeed real.

Lastly, feel the energy flow down into your waiting hand, energizing it, and taking over the muscles inside. At this point in the exercise, some individuals feel their hands begin to move, others will have to wait until they have opened their eyes and focused softly on the paper in front of them before they sense movement.

Step 10: Open Your Eyes—Soft Focus

In order to go on to the next phase of Automatic Writing you must open your eyes or you could be left with a jumbled mess of scribbles on your paper that you won't be able to decipher later.

This step can be a problem even for experienced Automatic Writers, as opening one's eyes while in a trance tends to be somewhat jarring. The trick is to open your eyes slowly, and then only part way. You want to have a soft, dreamy, half-awake focus that won't bring you up from your altered state of consciousness but will still allow you the use of your vision.

If you find you are one of many who initially have difficulty with this step, dim the lights in your work room, still allowing yourself to see the paper in front of you. Or you can try working by candlelight. These soft lights are not as jarring to the newly-opened eye as are fluorescent or incandescent bulbs, and can make the transition easier.

Step 11: Write!

If you do not feel your hand begin to move of its own volition, do not be discouraged. For many of us it takes time to reach the state where the words just pour forth as from a broken dam. Begin by writing down any impressions that come to mind; this often triggers the automatic reaction you are looking for.

You may also feel the urge to sketch or draw, especially if you are a visually oriented person. Allow these images to flow through your pen just as you would allow the words to come. Sometimes these picture symbols can convey more potent meanings than their verbal counterparts.

Step 12: Come Out of Meditative State

When you feel you have received all the communication you want for one session, or it has stopped of its own volition, or you have decided for yourself to stop and try again later, you need to bring yourself out of your meditative state. The best way to do this is by reversing whatever process you used to bring yourself into it. For instance, if you counted down, try counting up. If you merely relaxed, then feel yourself slowly tensing. If you focused on a candle, then open your eyes and focus on it again.

Allow yourself time to feel the renewed tension of your life force, the involuntary physical sensations of your living body, to remember what it is you are doing and where you are, and then open your eyes wide and go about your business.

Do this step completely, even though you are anxious to read what you have written. You took the time to properly take yourself down, and you need that same time to properly bring yourself up. Recall how disoriented and fatigued you felt on a day when you woke up too quickly from a sound night's sleep. This is the same unpleasant sensation you will have if you come out of your meditative state too quickly. The only exception to this would be if you were suddenly faced with an emergency that required your immediate attention. Again, the marvelous human mind can compensate for so many things. We have all been amazed at how people who are drugged, drunk, or sound asleep are often able to quickly sober up and jump into action when they have to, and so will you if an unforeseen problem arises while you are in an altered state of consciousness.

Step 13: Ground Yourself

It is also sound practice to "ground" yourself when you are finished. This is simply a means to re-establish your link with the earth plane, the plane of consciousness where we all live our day-to-day lives.

This can easily be achieved by grounding the excess energy from your chakras into the earth, as outlined in the previous chapter. You can ring a bell, clap your hands, or shout, since loud, sharp noises always work. You can also do something physical such as eating (particularly a salty food), or by going to the bathroom. Do whatever it takes to make you feel wide awake and functioning in your normal consciousness.

Step 14: Ground Your Protection

It is standard occult practice to ground any protective energies you may raise for a special ritual such as using Automatic Writing. If you raised a circle then you should ground it by mentally sending the energy into the earth and retracing your steps counter-clockwise, or widdershins. Sweep up any herbs you may have scattered or else mentally allow their energy to seep into the ground. Put away all amulets or talismans, and thank and dismiss any protective beings you called upon during prayers or other evocations you may have done beforehand.

If you find yourself unsure of how to ground a protection energy, just think of how you might reverse the process you took to create it and you cannot go wrong.

Some people fear that after they finish their Automatic Writing that their writing hand may be taken over by some outside force and compelled to write when they don't want to do so. They fear that if they let go of their protection that they are opening themselves up to trouble. While there have been claims of such incidents happening, they are exceedingly rare. However, if this is a concern for you, after you have grounded your protection, you can create a binding ritual.

A binding ritual is an old magickal art that binds an object to a single person. In this case, it would bind your hand to you. They are very effective and should lay to rest any fears you have. Of course, you must use caution when attempting any binding effort. The implications of the Pagan axiom, "As ye bind, so are ye bound" must be considered. You don't want to bind your hand so deeply to the material world that it can never freely and fully function for you as a medium between the worlds of form and spirit.

Many old magickal grimoires have binding spells in them, some simple and others complex. If you do not have one that you like, you can use one of the following:

Binding Ritual/Spell No. 1

To begin, you will need a long piece of light-weight cotton thread, a small piece of paper, a pen or pencil, and a candle.

Sit in front of the candle flame and draw a picture of your hand with your pencil and paper.

Visualize it as being wholly a part of you and under your complete control. This visualized energy is more important than how well you actually can draw.

Next, make a fist with your writing hand and wrap the thread around your fist, binding it together. Don't wrap it too tightly or you will have trouble when it comes to burning it off. The thread represents both your fear and any negative energy which you fear will take over your hand, and you must now release that fear by allowing the purifying force of the candle flame to burn through the bonds of fear which hold you (Be careful not to burn yourself!).

As your hand is released, feel it being returned fully to your control. Now pick up the pieces of thread and wrap them tightly around the picture you drew of your hand.

As you do this visualize yourself in charge of the binding; you are now taking control of your hand. Often people like to chant a charm to seal the spell. Try something like this:

> *By this flame and this thread's band,*
> *To me is bound the mystic hand.*

When the picture is tightly wrapped, put it in a safe place such as a dresser drawer. As long as you have this talisman, you should be free from any negative interference when you are not willingly doing Automatic Writing.

Binding Ritual/Spell No. 2

To begin, you will need to buy or make a poppet, a small doll that will represent you. It need not be anything fancy. Two pieces of cloth cut into a human shape, sewn together and stuffed with cotton will do. As you make the poppet you should invest as much personal energy into it as you can. See the doll as being an extension of yourself. If you choose to buy a doll instead, you should make it a part of you by carrying it around with you for several days, coming into physical contact with it as much as possible, investing it with your personal energy.

You will also need to have a piece of heavy thread, preferably in black, and a pen or marker.

After you are finished with your Automatic Writing, sit down with the poppet. Take hold of the writing hand and, with your breath, blow from it any negative influences. Feel these being carried far away from you.

With the marker, inscribe on the hand a symbol of protection that has meaning to you.

Now bind the writing arm of the poppet to its body by taking the thread in counter-clockwise motions around the body of the doll.

As you do this, see the hand as being fully bound to you—part of you, always under your control. As you wrap the thread, you can chant a poem to help strengthen your visualization:

> *Hand of mine,*
> *To me I bind.*
> *Only my will*
> *Can move the quill.*

When you are finished, put the poppet some place safe where only you can find it. As long as it is in your possession you should be free of any negative interference when not willingly doing your Automatic Writing.

Step 15: Keep Records

This final step in successful Automatic Writing is one so many novices—and some experienced folks who should know better—often overlook. I cannot over-emphasize the importance of keeping good records of your Automatic Writing. The cryptic message that is not clear today may make profound sense in a month or so and become very important to you.

When you are finished with Step 14, make an initial assessment of your writing immediately. Write down any first impressions of the messages, notes on your feelings about it, or sensations you had while writing it. Often your first gut reaction is the best, especially if you need to decode passages of seeming gibberish.

You should also make notes on the day of the week and the time of day you wrote, noting weather conditions and astrological influences you feel might be of importance. Later, if you run into stumbling blocks that inhibit your Automatic Writing abilities, you can look for patterns in these conditions and possibly discover the best time for you to work, the time when you are most psychically potent and sensitive.

Pick one day a month to go back through your writing and look for new insights. I like to choose the day of the new moon because of its symbolic association with new beginnings, but any date which you can easily remember is the best to pick. You may be astounded at what fresh perspectives on situations this hindsight can reveal, and over time this practice will also better help you assess your current writings.

I find that the best record-keeping book is a large loose-leaf notebook. You can easily attach new pages of writing as they are made, and you can add, remove, condense, or expand the pages of your commentary as events come and go in your life.

As you gain more confidence in this art, you will eventually be able to interact more with it, rather than passively receiving messages. You can carry on dialogue, ask for clarification of flowery language or obscure passages, and even change topics in midstream.

Again, the greatest so-called "secret" of successful Automatic Writing is practice, practice, practice.

❦ ❧

The 15 Steps
for Successful
Automatic Writing

1. Gather your equipment.
2. Go to your work place.
3. Clear your work area.
4. Protect yourself.
5. Write out your question.
6. Place yourself in a meditative state.
7. Bring energy into your chakras.
8. Focus on your question.
9. Bring the energy into your writing arm.
10. Open your eyes—soft focus.
11. Write!
12. Come out of meditative state.
13. Ground yourself.
14. Ground your protection.
15. Keep records.

❦ ❧

❧ 7 ❧

If at First You Don't Succeed....

If you have faithfully followed all the instructions in this book and still have not found success, you may need to allow yourself the full sixty days to work on these techniques. During this time practice your Automatic Writing each and every day, at the same time if possible. This repetition helps condition your mind as to what you are expecting of it. Just like you expect it to fall into sleep at a certain time and tell you you are hungry at another, it can be trained to know when it's time to do Automatic Writing. Try not to skip a single day or you will lose a little of what you have gained. Be sure to keep up with the chakra exercises, too.

There are other exercises you can do to help make your mind more receptive and your environment more conducive to any psychic work, Automatic Writing included. Many of these are elaborated upon here. Find the ones that speak to you and use them faithfully while clearly visualizing your goal.

Automatic Drawing

Don't fight the urge to draw! Some people get so hung up on the word "writing" that they fight the picture symbols forming in their minds and ignore their compulsion to work them out on paper. Often these pictures can be much more potent than words, and can cut to the heart of an issue in a way that an entire tome could not.

If the channeled information in an Automatic Writing session comes to you in the form of pictures and you feel moved to sketch, you should allow it to happen. You may find this happens quite frequently, especially if you are artistically talented or have a visually-oriented mind. Sometimes these images will come alone, and sometimes they will present themselves along with a text as a means of clarification.

Automatic Drawing is less well-known, but is certainly a valid expression of the Collective Unconscious. If you feel you wish to explore this means of automatic communication, or feel you would be more successful with it than with words, you can prepare yourself for it by having in your hand a piece of charcoal, a paintbrush, or whatever medium you enjoy working in artistically. As you channel down the energy of the Collective Unconscious, tell yourself that you wish to have your answers come in the form of pictures. Then simply allow it to happen. Begin moving your hand in a drawing motion, allowing any pictures that form in your mind to flow onto your paper. Also, don't fight the urge to place words or labels on drawings if the idea comes to you.

As with Automatic Writing, when you become proficient, you should be able to switch mediums in midstream, use different paints, etc., and create scenes rich with symbolism.

Keep in mind when you begin to interpret this Automatic Drawing that the pictures you create will not always be "normal," but will contain potent archetypal symbols you will have to sort out when you are finished. This will be somewhat more difficult than interpreting your writing, but will be worth the effort. Look at how each part of the picture relates to the whole, at the size of each in comparison to the other, and study the boldness of each stroke. Even the color(s) you feel compelled to use can have a lot to say about the message being sent. See the archetypes guide in Chapter Nine for more help in learning to interpret these messages.

Lastly, don't ever feel you have failed at Automatic Writing if all your communication comes in pictures. Some people are just visually-oriented. If you find your Automatic Drawing helpful, then that is all that matters.

Using The Pen

For many of us it takes time and practice to reach the state where the words pour forth from our pens. Fortunately there are several tricks you can use to push the process along.

Trick #1: Keep your neck straight

Your natural tendency will be to crane your neck over your paper so that you can better see what is going on. But seeing any more of the paper than where it is and where your hand is flowing is not really necessary. Bending your neck can impede the flow of energy you need to keep your Automatic Writing moving; it can cause a tension in your body that can jolt you out of your altered state, and it can force you to concentrate too hard on the mechanics of your endeavor rather than on the question or issue at hand.

Trick #2: Detach from the process

Often you might feel a tingling in your hand or a sensation of slight movement and you become so excited that you inadvertently bring yourself up out of the relaxed meditative state you need in order to work. As difficult as it may be, you must force yourself not to become overly eager when the writing begins to happen. The famous English magician Aleister Crowley put it best when he called this emotion "will-less will." You can't let yourself become totally disinterested in what is happening, but neither can you allow yourself to really experience it while it is occurring. Rather you need to let it come as if you were watching it happen to someone else. Relax for now and save the celebration and elation for later.

Fear can be a powerful energy inhibitor. Often when the hand begins writing on its own, the novice Automatic Writer becomes afraid and the process comes to a grinding halt. Learning to emotionally detach yourself from the actual writing process will also help prevent fear from impeding your progress.

Trick #3: Write down your random thoughts

Don't discount random impressions. Allow yourself to be aware of any impressions that enter your mind at this time, especially if you want to disregard them and find you can't. This can often be the start of your first automatic communication. It was this way for me.

Trick #4: Don't stop to analyze

If you do get your pen moving with a communication, be it automatic or a series of random impressions, do not try to judge them for the time being. Critical analysis at this point might bring you out of your meditative state or halt the energy flow that is feeding your communication. You have the rest of your life to think about the written words, for now just let them happen.

Trick #5: Keep writing in a legible fashion

Some people who teach this process tell you to make doodle marks on your paper in order to get your pen moving. However, I have found that most doodles do not follow the natural flow of normal writing and can actually impede your progress. Instead of doodling, you should write something real. Write your name over and over if necessary, write the name of the entity you wish to contact, or write the word WRITE. Do whatever makes you write legible words on your paper, rather than useless swirls, doodles, or lines.

This process can use up a lot of paper before you actually begin writing. In this case it might be good to have extra sheets of paper near at hand. If this is your first time trying Automatic Writing, or if you find you consistently have to use this trick, you may want to keep extra paper nearby.

Herbal Help

Magickal herbalism is the art of using the energies found in natural things to align you with your goals and desires. In this case you would want to use those herbs known for enhancing psychic work. Their power can be harnessed in many forms including incenses, teas, bath additives, or as items that you can carry with you.

Incenses have been used since ancient times to aid psychic work, help individuals petition their deities, to align a person's energies with their magickal goals, to flavor rituals, or to help simple concentration. Many incenses can be bought commercially either in cones or joss sticks. If you cannot find the scents you want in stores or through mail order houses, or if the ones you do find are not of high quality, you can make your own by tossing a small handful of the raw herbs onto smoldering coals placed in a fireproof censer.

Incenses particularly suited to aiding Automatic Writing are those traditionally associated with opening the psychic centers or with the planets of Mercury (which govern communication and writing) or the Moon (which governs psychicism). Try using incenses of cedar, rosemary, sandalwood, copal, cinnamon, frankincense, peppermint, honeysuckle, or lavender.

Many people have a number they feel is lucky for them, or one which is sacred to their religious tradition, and they wish to incorporate it into their Automatic Writing. Feel free to mix these herbal scents, in the right number, into custom incenses. For example, if your tradition says

seven is lucky, then blend together seven different herbs in your incense. Remember, the mixture doesn't have to smell good. It just has to
work. However, if you are sensitive to odors,
then it is a good idea to find an incense you like
or it will distract.

Teas are probably the easiest way to harness
the power of herbs. About an hour before you
wish to do an Automatic Writing, relax and drink
a tea, or mixture of teas, known to aid psychic
work. Be aware that many of these teas can make
you a bit drowsy, so be sure you don't have to
work or drive soon after using them.

The teas best suited for aiding your Automatic Writing are not always the ones that taste
good. Work with them to get a blend you like, or
at least one you can tolerate. Try one or any mixture of catnip, valerian, red clover, white oak
bark, hyssop, vanilla bean, heather, seaweed,
chamomile, vervain, bistort, eyebright, mugwort,
lemongrass, or saffron.

Use one heaping teaspoon of herbs for each
cup of tea you wish to make. Steep them in hot
water by using a tea ball, or place them in the filter of your coffee maker.

Valerian is, in my opinion, one of the best
psychic enhancers that exists. However, it has
three drawbacks: it can make you quite sleepy; it
is mildly addictive if used constantly; and, it

smells awful. If you wish to use this herb and feel you can stay awake long enough to work with it, try adding a generous amount of peppermint herbs to the tea to cut the strong odor and taste.

Anise and jasmine are almost as good as valerian, and are more pleasant to drink. If you want to try other tea options following are herbal tea combinations known to be psychic enhancers:

• Valerian, catnip, peppermint

• Jasmine, anise

• Mugwort, hibiscus, orris root, dandelion

• Red clover, catnip

• Catnip, rosemary

• Buchu, jasmine, mugwort

• Cinquefoil, bistort, lemongrass

• Honeysuckle, peppermint, lemongrass

• Saffron, jasmine

• Balm of Gilead, peppermint, cinnamon

• Ginseng, vervain, catnip

• Anise, peppermint, bistort

• Balm of Gilead, anise, red clover, rosemary

• Chamomile, red clover

• Vervain, mugwort

Herbs can also be tossed into a bathtub where you can soak up their energies. Be sure to visualize your goal of success as you soak. The herbal bath can also have the desired effect of helping you relax and mentally preparing you for the work ahead. Wrap the herbs beforehand in cheesecloth to prevent clogging the drain.

You can also carry herbs with you that you have poured your own energy into (this is always the best way to use the herbs that can be dangerous or toxic to inhale or drink). Charge your chosen herbs by holding them in your projective hand (the one you write with) and visualizing your goal. Feel your needs and concerns pouring into the herb and blending with its own energies. You can hold onto the herbs while you write or, better still, stick them in a pocket.

Many common herbs have other properties besides psychic enhancement. You can also use them to help you focus and/or align yourself with a specific question or issue by using any of the above mentioned methods (or as essential oils, described after the herb list). The following is a list of some common herbs and their associated properties. If the need or herb you are looking for is not listed, check the "Suggested Reading" section in the back of this book for the names of books that contain more comprehensive herbal information:

Herb	Associated Energies
Acacia	Psychic enhancer, protection
Agrimony	Romance, dreams
Alfalfa	Fertility, prosperity
Allspice	Protection, health, wish making
Anise	Psychic enhancer, protection
Apple	Divination, Romance, Health
Aspen	Protection
Balm of Gilead	Psychic enhancer, dream work
Barley	Fertility, prosperity, employment
Basil	Protection, astral work
Bay	Psychic enhancer, protection, health
Bistort	Fertility, psychic enhancer, binding
Bladderwrack	Psychic enhancer
Boneset	Health, legal matters, binding
Buchu	Psychic enhancer, dream work
Burdock	Protection, health, clear thinking
Camphor	Protection, psychic enhancer
Catnip	Psychic enhancer, general magick aid
Chamomile	Psychic enhancer, romance, dream work
Cinnamon	Protection, money, lust, power
Cinquefoil	Protection, prosperity, divination
Clove	Protection, prosperity
Clover	Peace, fidelity, appearance, romance

Herb	Associated Energies
Comfrey	Matters of travel, prosperity
Dandelion	Spirit contact, divination
Dill	Protection, lust, money
Echinacea	General magic aid, health
Eucalyptus	Health, protection
Eyebright	Divination, dream work
Fennel	Protection
Fenugreek	Money, employment, leadership
Feverfew	Health, binding
Frankincense	Protection, money
Garlic	Protection, health, lust
Ginger	Protection, success booster, romance
Ginseng	Psychic enhancer, protection
Goldenrod	Psychic enhancer, protection
Gotukola	Meditation, mental power
Hazel	Protection, fertility, wish-making
Heather	Spiritual enhancer, protection
Hibiscus	Romance, lust, personal power
Hyssop	Protection, health, concentration
Irish Moss	Dream work, matters of children
Jasmine	Psychic enhancer, dream work, peace
Lavender	Spirit contact, divination, romance

Herb	Associated Energies
Lemongrass	Psychic enhancer, protection
Lilac	Travel, past lives, astral work
Linden	Protection
Lotus	Psychic enhancer
Marjoram	Protection, psychic enhancer
Mugwort	Astral work, psychic cleansing
Mullein	Courage, protection, divination, love
Myrtle	Appearance, romance, peace, money
Nettle	Protection, banishing, lust, health
Oak	Strength, fertility, protection
Oats	Fertility, prosperity
Orris	Psychic enhancer, romance, divination
Parsley	Protection
Passion Flower	Psychic enhancer, lust, divination
Patchouly	Fertility, lust, grounding
Pipsissewa	Divination, past lives
Potato	Stability, fertility, grounding
Pepper	Protection, banishing
Pine	Money, prosperity, fertility, health
Purslane	Dream work, astral work, happiness
Ragwort	Protection, astral work

Herb	Associated Energies
Rice	Fertility, good luck, money
Rosemary	Protection, mental powers, romance
Rowan	Psychic enhancer, protection, binding
Rue	Protection, mental powers, banishing
Sandalwood	Protection, peace, wish making
Saffron	Divination, general magic aid, love
Sage	Mental powers, divination
Skullcap	Fertility, romance, peace, good luck
Spearmint	Psychic enhancer, healing, protection
Straw	Prosperity, good luck
Thistle	Protection, health, banishing, dreams
Thyme	Protection, psychic enhancer
Turmeric	Protection, psychic cleansing
Vervain	Romance, fidelity, protection
Willow	Personal strength, love, divination
Wintergreen	Health, protection, banishing
Yarrow	Psychic enhancer, protection, love
Yucca	Protection

A final word of caution: Be sure that if you are using herbs of questionable safety that you do not leave them where they can be found by children or pets. All of the herbs mentioned in this guide are generally thought to be safe, but some may cause you problems through skin irritations or other allergic reactions. Always approach any unfamiliar substance with caution.

Essential Oils

Essential oils are the oils pressed from living plants, and are very concentrated and often volatile. If you wish to use these, it is best to first dilute them in a scentless and non-irritating oil such as olive or safflower. Use only three or four drops of the essential oil to about one ounce of the diluting medium. You can keep these fresh for several months in jars that are kept out of light, or, better still, in dark eye-dropper bottles purchased at your local pharmacy.

Even when diluted you should use essential oils sparingly, placing one single drop on your Third Eye area. Not only will the oil stimulate this psychic center, but the potent scent will act like an incense and help set your mind to your task while blocking out everyday distracting scents.

Oils to enhance your Automatic Writing are tuberose, lilac, rosemary, jasmine, sandalwood, honeysuckle, and lotus. Clove and cinnamon oils are also good psychic catalysts, and they can be placed on the paper you are writing on, but you should avoid putting them on yourself because they will irritate the skin.

Some oils have long been known to aid certain goals such as past-life regression. For example, it has been an accepted practice to place a drop of lilac oil on each temple and on the Third Eye when seeking past-life insights. Rosemary oil can be used to seek information on healing, romance, or intellectual matters. Sandalwood or jasmine oil will raise your spiritual vibrations and help you attune to them.

A few drops of these diluted oils can also be added to bath water where you can sit and soak up their energies. Be sure to visualize your success as you bathe.

Essential oils also release their power through scent. This is called aromatherapy, and is an especially useful tool if your skin is sensitive. To use aromatherapy, simply take the vial of your chosen oil to your working spot and open it up, allowing it to release its fragrance throughout the room. If the bottled scent is too weak for your tastes, you can enhance it by placing some out on a cotton ball, by anointing a burning candle, or by putting just a single drop on a warm light bulb. Spend a few moments before you start writing doing deep breathing exercises while visualizing your goal.

Talismans

Psychic enhancing talismans can be made of any of the raw herbs mentioned. Choose the ones you like, tie them together in a small cloth, and carry them on you when you do your writing. Instructions for making these sachets, commonly called Totem Bags, are found in Chapter Six.

You can also add to the talisman any other objects that represent your goal. Cut out magazine pictures, find a stone or twig that speaks to you of psychic power, insert copies of other success stories, write out the name of a famous medium you admire. Be creative!

Stone Help

Stones are perhaps the oldest amulets known to humankind. Our ancestors no doubt picked up interesting rocks as they went on their nomadic wanderings. After a while they began to notice subtle but certain advantages of each type of stone, and thus the art of stone magick was born.

Before you use any stone for a magical purpose you should first "program" it by holding it in your projective hand (the one you write with) and spend some time visually projecting into it your need and how you wish it to help you. The clearer you can visualize this, the better programmed the stone will be. With repeated use, the stone will work better and better because it will absorb and align itself with your energy and the energy of your efforts.

The energy of any of these charged stones can be transferred to you by wearing them as jewelry, placing them in a pocket, holding them in your non-writing hand, or bathing with them. Unlike herbs, stones don't seem to be able to do their job as well from a distance. Allowing them to touch you in some way is the best method for aligning yourself with their energies.

Like herbs, different stones have specific energies, some of which are very attuned to enhancing psychic work such as Automatic Writing. Stones best suited for this are white, silver, blue, or violet in color. Quartz crystals are also useful as they are an excellent catalyst for psychic energy. Diamonds, lodestones, and opals are also good to try.

If your purpose in doing Automatic Writing is spiritual rather than material in nature, you might try using a turquoise. This elegant blue-green stone has been used by Native Americans for many centuries to enhance spirituality and to help them connect with the powers of their benevolent spirits.

Stones, like herbs, also have particular affinities, and these can be used if you know specifically what your question will be. For example, a rose quartz has long been associated with romantic love and would be a good one to wear if your question is one of romance. Below is a list of the energy associations of some of the more popular stones and gems. If what you are looking for isn't here, check the "Suggested Reading" section on Page 259 to find other books that can help you find the right stone for your purposes.

The Stone	Associated Energies
Agate, Blue	Addictions, obsessions
Agate, Brown	Animals
Agate, Green	Prosperity, jealousy
Alexandrite	Protection, health
Amber	Beauty
Amethyst	Psychicism, dreams
Aquamarine	Peace, psychicism
Black Onyx	Dreams, psychicism, illness
Bloodstone	Fertility, fairness, marriage
Carnelian	Anger, passion, justice, protection
Coral	Children, the home
Citrine	Divination, protection
Diamond	All Needs

The Stone	Associated Energies
Emerald	Money, prosperity, beauty, fertility
Flint	Protection
Fluorite	Health
Garnet	Health, courage, fair judgment
Geodes	Fertility, meditation
Golden Topaz	Employment, money, protection
Granite	Protection, fidelity, grounding
Hematite	Health, grounding
Holey Stones	Fertility
Jade	Psychicism, money, balance, fertility
Jasper, Green	Prosperity
Jasper, Yellow	Protection
Jasper, Red	Strength, protection, lust
Lava	Grounding, protection
Lapis Lazuli	Domestic affairs, travel
Lodestone	Psychicism, attraction, binding
Malachite	Animals, prosperity
Meteorite	Astral projection, travel
Mica	Additions, psychicism
Moonstone	Psychicism, motherhood, women
Obsidian	Psychicism, dreams, the hidden
Opal	All needs
Pearl	Psychicism, dreams, romance
Peridot	Money, treachery
Quartz Crystal	Excellent energy catalyst
Sapphire	Peace, dreams
Rhodocrosite	Divination, raising energy

The Stone	Associated Energies
Rose Quartz	Romance, peace
Ruby	Passion, lust, conflict, protection
Tiger's Eye	Personal power, protection
Tourmaline	Passion, marriage, protection
Turquoise	All spiritual endeavors
Zircon	All needs

Music to Soothe

The right kind of music can help you focus on your goal while blocking out noises that might break your concentration. But not all music is suited to this task.

Most New Age music is written to have little or no cadence which might disturb someone attempting to place themselves in an altered state of consciousness. It is structured so that the meter, or time system on which all music is hung, is not readily noticed. Such music is usually written specifically for meditation. Look for labels marked "inner-harmony" or "inner-journey" music to make sure you have what you need. (Two labels that are especially good are Narvada and Valley of the Sun.)

If you look through your own collection of recorded music you might be surprised to find that you have several selections to use. Any music without a driving beat could work. Avoid any music with specific memories or emotional connections as they could color your writing. The music played on "easy listening" radio stations is also worth experimenting with.

If you are musically talented you can write and record your own meditation music. Keep it soothing, allowing chord progressions to flow naturally, but to rarely resolve themselves on the tonic chord. Listen critically to other New Age music to get additional ideas.

If you are easily distracted by mundane noises, use headphones as you write.

The Power of Color

You have learned how the colored energies of the chakras can aid your Automatic Writing, but you should also know that there are other color energies that can help you.

Modern psychology has recently discovered what occultists have known for centuries, that different colors have the power to alter one's mind and moods. You can harness the power of color to help your Automatic Writing.

To use color in your Automatic Writing endeavors you can burn colored candles, add the color to your clothing, make it into a tablecloth, or add it to the room you use in the form of draperies, paint, or wallpaper. The choice is yours, just be sure it is one you can live with if you drastically alter your room.

Avoid red at all costs (unless you are working with planetary energies, discussed in Chapter Four). Red is the color of action and excitement. Studies have shown that individuals in red rooms develop a slightly elevated blood pressure, they become irritable more quickly, and they usually overestimate the time they spend in the room. In other words, it is too much of a stimulant for your pursuits.

While orange shares some of red's attributes, it is a color associated with communication and its ruling planet Mercury. Orange may help you focus on your goal.

Yellow is the color of the stimulated intellect and can also be useful, unless you associate it solely with scholarly pursuits.

Green is a tranquil color, a color predominant in nature, but it is more conducive to ritual than to psychic endeavors.

Blue is also tranquil. Studies have shown that blue rooms can help lower blood pressure, and people often underestimate the amount of time spent in them. However, excessive time around blue can be depressing. Blue is also the color of the Throat Chakra and is therefore associated with communication.

Indigo and violet are also soothing, but can be overpowering to the psyche in large doses. They are the colors of the Third Eye and Crown Chakras, respectively, and are associated with psychicism and the Higher Self. They are excellent choices to use during Automatic Writing.

Silver is a color long associated with psychicism in occult circles. It is the color of the moon, the planet that governs psychic work. Some people even prefer to visualize their Crown Chakra in this color. Silver jewelry may help your efforts.

Gold is associated with the energy of the sun and you may use it if you feel a need to step up the power of your personal energy, but it has little use as a psychic enhancement.

Pink is associated with romantic love and would be a good color to choose when doing a reading for your mate or seeking information on any issues relating to romance.

All these color attributes are merely suggestions. We all have our own inner color schedule that has nothing to do with clinical studies or occult custom. For example, if someone you loathed always dressed in purple, and you associate that color with them, it would not be a good choice for your Automatic Writing efforts.

Candle Power

People have used the warm golden glow of candlelight for many centuries to aid psychic work. There are two ways in which candles can help you learn Automatic Writing.

If you are attracted to the gentle fire of candles, it might be a smart idea to practice your writing in a darkened room with only the flame of one or several candles illuminating the page in front of you. It seems like a small act, but it is just the sort of trigger that often stimulates the deep mind into action. Choose candle colors that speak to you of opening the psychic channels. White, silver, gold, and violet are the colors most commonly chosen.

If you are having trouble opening your eyes without feeling jolted out of your meditative state, focus on a candle flame in a dimly lit room instead of closing your eyes completely. Choose a neutral colored candle for this exercise. Keep it far enough away that staring at it won't hurt your eyes, and be sure to keep your gaze in the same soft focus you will use when you are writing. Concentrate solely on your question and let the single dancing flame take you down into your altered state.

When you feel you are down where you need to be, gently transfer your gaze to the paper in front of you. You will see the glaring image of the candlelight on the page, but this will fade in a minute or so. However, if the words begin to come, don't wait for your sight to clear. Write anyway and save reading it for later.

Never leave a burning candle unattended, and keep it well out of reach of drapes, matches, or other flammable items. Also take the time to invest in good candleholders. Holders that are too small will allow wax to drip everywhere, and those that are too light for the candle can cause it to tip over. Wooden holders will burn when the candle melts down to their level, and ones made of thin metal can cause the surface beneath to scorch.

The Power of Nature

Some people find that no matter how quiet and comfortable their homes are, they just cannot get into a receptive frame of mind while inside. This is especially true for people who have large families, who work in their homes, or have phones that are always ringing.

Experiment with natural settings for your Automatic Writing. Go deep into the woods, sit in the grass of your own backyard, or drive out into the country until you find a field of wildflowers. You can use a friendly tree or large stone outcropping to help support your back. Just make sure your surroundings will be quiet and private.

You can also use nature to get you into a proper frame of mind before you begin writing. Talk a long walk under a full moon, swim a few vigorous laps in the local swimming hole, sit on the banks of the local lake and listen to the frogs croaking, or stroll through a full-blooming spring garden or greenhouse. All these natural sights and sounds will help sharpen your senses and make you more receptive.

Using Other Oracles To Get You Started

Oracles at which you are already proficient, such as the Tarot cards or the Runes, can also be enlisted to help you start Automatic Writing. If you are accustomed to their language they can be used to help you concentrate. Because your mind is already keyed to their powerful symbols, focusing on one of them can help transfer their divinatory power into this new oracle, and, at the same time help your deep mind, which communicates with symbols, understand that you need its aid to translate these picture symbols to written ones.

To begin, pick one card or Rune stone that has meaning for you or for your effort. For example, if you are working with Tarot cards you might want to choose the Magician for his archetypal ability to bring ideas into the being. Set your chosen object in front of you, level with your eyes, much as you would use a candle. Focus your eyes softly on it as you take yourself into a meditative state of mind. When the time is right, transfer your gaze to your paper and begin to write.

The added symbology of another familiar oracle is often a powerful trigger for your mind to help you get started.

A Psychic Diet

Some occultists say you should never attempt a psychic endeavor on a full stomach. Some go so far as to advocate a twenty-four hour fast before any such work, or suggest that you should permanently avoid certain "earthy" foods like whole grains or meat. Only you can decide how stringently you wish to follow this advice, and keep in mind that for people with certain medical conditions fasting can be dangerous.

An intelligent approach to a psychic diet that would get your Automatic Writing moving would be one that eliminated salt within a twenty-four hour period of your working. Salt is known to be very grounding and is often consumed to help individuals re-orient to earthly reality after a psychic working. Meat can also inhibit your energy flow and should be avoided until you achieve your goal. Needless to say, anything stimulating such as caffeine will not help you relax and fall into the proper meditative state.

There are no known foods or food combinations that have been consistently recommended for those engaged in psychic work, but if you want to use diet to aid you and you don't want to fast, eat vegetables and fruits, and drink fruit juices and/or purified water.

A Crown for Your Crown

The symbology of the crown as one of rulership comes from the ancient belief that the head is the seat of all human power—the place where the earth plane can connect with the all-knowing, all-seeing powers of the divine. Royalty wore crowns to show that they were sovereign and to signify their special rank as the chosen of the deities, and to help stimulate their connection to these beings.

You can wear something similar to help stimulate the powers of your Crown Chakra. Anything you feel will enhance the energy of this space is fine. Those involved in earth religions might want to use an item as simple as a daisy chain made into a chaplet. Persons involved in Ceremonial Magick might choose their ritual order's headdress. Tiaras or crowns won in contests are also acceptable if they speak to the user of personal power and achievement.

It is best not to use a head covering that completely covers the head. It can impede the actual energy flow, and your perception of it.

Auto-Suggestion

Auto-suggestion is a less technical term for self-hypnosis, and is a method by which the subconscious is conditioned by a word or phrase to manifest an action or to alter reality. Most New Age stores and occult shops sell a variety of audio tapes with subliminal messages in order to achieve this end, but you can effectively utilize these techniques for yourself without leaving your home.

To make auto-suggestion work for you, simply place yourself into a meditative state of consciousness and repeat a positive, present-tense affirmation over and over to yourself such as "I am good at Automatic Writing," "My Automatic Writing is very successful," or "Automatic Writing works for me."

Whatever affirmation you choose, make sure it is constructed in the present tense. This is another time-honored piece of occult wisdom. You are attempting to change your current conditions so you should always say things as if they are already a part of your present reality. Voicing desires in the future tense will forever keep them in your future, always out of your grasp.

Another way to make auto-suggestion work is by sitting in front of a mirror in a darkened room and repeating the phrase to your reflection as if you are another person speaking to yourself, kind of like a friend who is cheering you on. People who have trouble making clear visualizations often prefer this method.

The best times to do this are upon waking and before going to sleep. At these times your mind is naturally in a fuzzy world between wakefulness and sleep which is the essence of an altered state. Take advantage of it.

If you have the equipment and inclination to make your own subliminal tapes you can imbed these suggestions in music and play them whenever you have the time. While some people argue that subliminal messages only work because we think they work, this should not bother you if this is what you enjoy working with. If we think they work, they do work.

Remember that the idea of this exercise is to convince your deep mind that a desired reality is, in fact, already your reality, thereby enlisting its help to manifest the desired change. For best results, keep these exercises upbeat and never doubt their ultimate effectiveness.

Using A Sturdy Working Surface

Most people who practice Automatic Writing like to balance their notepad on their knees. This is fine for experienced people, but if you are having trouble breaking into the practice, you need a more solid surface to support your tablet and to keep your arms from tiring.

A flat surface such as a kitchen table or desk would be your best choice. You can even pull a chair or stool up to a dresser top or a kitchen counter if no other space is available. Be sure to cleanse and purify the surface with water mixed with a bit of mugwort herb, salt water, incense, or oil to remove unwanted vibrations and influences from it before you begin working. This is especially important if others regularly touch or use your chosen work surface.

Believe In Yourself and Be Realistic

Never doubt for a moment that you have inside yourself all the answers you need to function happily and healthily. Too many people fail with divination—Automatic Writing included—because they always feel someone else must know them better than they know themselves, or that someone else has some great talent they themselves lack. This idea is reinforced when instant solutions to long-term problems don't jump off the page at them. They give up or, worse yet, start doubting themselves. I have seen too many money-hungry charlatans encouraging this line of thinking and charging as much as $150 for a simple psychic reading. Anyone can buy a divination device and instruction book for under $25—the same tools the so-called psychic charging you learned from.

Others may learn Automatic Writing faster than you and appear to work more smoothly, but no one can really help you as well as you.

Also, make sure your expectations are realistic. If your writing works for you eight out of the ten times you sit down to use it, then you are doing very well. You will have off days with your occult endeavors, like anything else you undertake. Sometimes you may not feel well, or may have trouble concentrating, or for reasons you may never know, things just aren't connecting. This is normal. Anyone who tells you differently is either bragging or lying. Don't let an off day worry you, merely accept it and try again later.

And please keep in mind, no matter how good you become, no one can know all the great secrets of the universe, not you, and not some expensive psychic. Don't expect to become as omniscient as a God with Automatic Writing. If you can produce sound, helpful, and insightful readings for yourself and for others that offer guidance and comfort when you need it, then consider yourself a great success.

If You Still Have Troubles

If you have followed faithfully all the exercises and suggestions in this book and are still having trouble, you need to examine any blocks that may be inhibiting your progress. Reasons for these blocks commonly include such things as fear, disbelief in the practice, or a past memory of psychic work in which you were frightened or upset.

If you can discover no blockages or if you can work through them and still are not successful, you may need to find another method for this art or, even better, develop your own techniques. While there are similarities among all of these, there is no one single path to success. The practice I outline differs considerably from the one I was taught, and, in turn, everyone I have taught has made their own refinements. Experiment until you hit on the method that is right for you.

Also keep in mind that everyone learns and develops at different rates of speed. You may have learned to read quicker than your best friend. The same is true for occult endeavors. You may need more than sixty days of steady work in order to be successful.

❧ 8 ❧

Doing Automatic Writing For Others

Once it becomes general knowledge among your friends and family that you have mastered the art of Automatic Writing, you will be surprised by how many requests you get to do readings for them. Even your devoutly anti-occult old aunt may surprise you with her interest. "Reading" is another term for divination, and probably came from the idea of reading, or interpreting, the symbolic language of such devices as Tarot cards. The word is most commonly used in reference to doing a divination for someone else even when your "reading" is Automatic Writing.

Those practiced in the occult arts have long known that doing divinations for others has its drawbacks, particularly in that you are naturally distanced from your subject. After all, you are a separate entity from these other people, and your Higher Self, while able to gather a certain amount of information from others, is not overly anxious to do so because it sees no benefit to you. To successfully read for others you must make your

Higher Self care about them by giving it intimate knowledge of that person and their problem.

To put it simply, the secret to getting sound readings for other people is to establish either an emotional or physical link with them (and to do both is better yet).

If the Person is Present

If the person requesting a reading can be with you while you do your Automatic Writing you will be able to form a bond that will enable you to contact their Higher Self or possibly even their Spirit Guide. At the least, you may be able to gather psychic impressions from contact with their subconscious mind and gather buried information for them. You can form this bond either emotionally or physically.

Emotional Bonding

If you are emotionally close to this person in a positive way, and if you love him or her as a friend or relative, you have an advantage. If the person is a stranger, making an emotional connection is more difficult, but not impossible.

Before you begin the Automatic Writing have the person explain to you in detail what the problem is and why it is urgent that it be solved. This way you can share their concern, sadness, desires, and anxiety. An old maxim states that desire is half the component in successful occult practices.

If the person asking your help knows of a spirit or discarnate who might be able to help find the answers, he or she should tell you so that your Higher Self can begin to focus on this entity and attempt to make its own contact.

Laying your left hand (or your right if you are left handed) on their Heart Center Chakra for a few moments will also help you connect with their emotions.

Physical Bonding

If you feel you can go into a successful altered state of consciousness with someone in the room with you, you may allow the person asking your help to stay. It is even better if you can allow them to take your hand (not the one you write with).

Certain stones clasped between your palms can also help facilitate your mutual energy. Many people will choose a plain quartz crystal, but you are not limited. Established couples might choose to use a rose quartz, which is often seen as a stone of love, or even an engagement ring containing a diamond. Orange stones are associated with the powers of the planet Mercury and its affinity of communication. Yellow stones are associated with mental acuity, and shiny white stones with the psychic powers of the moon.

A less interruptive way to make a physical link is by breathing in unison. Allow yourselves to inhale deeply and rhythmically until you are both fully relaxed and in sync. Sometimes you will sense this has begun to work when you get random psychic impressions even before you begin to write. You don't need to write these down, but feel free to discuss them with your client afterwards, as they might prove useful.

If the Person is Not Present

If the person requesting a reading cannot be with you, there are ways to make an emotional or physical bond with them.

Emotional Bonding

Allow the person to explain their troubles in the same way you would ask them to do if they were in the room with you. This can be done over the phone or in a letter, but the information should be first-hand and not relayed through a third party. Allow yourself to feel all of their emotions and needs concerning their problem so that you can recall and connect with it prior to doing your Automatic Writing.

If the person is a close friend or family member you should call on all your good feelings toward him or her prior to your writing. Having a photograph of them handy is helpful in this case, particularly of the two of you when you were engaged in a happy event together. Wedding pictures, class pictures, and family reunion pictures are especially good for this because they readily call upon strong feelings.

Physical Bonding

Physical bonding with a person not present sounds impossible, but remember that all people have energy emanations and centers to link themselves temporarily to others.

One of the easiest and oldest known ways to connect with the energy of another person is by holding onto an object they have had contact with. This process of gleaning information from an inanimate object is called psychometry. Naturally, the more intimately connected your subject has been with the object, the more their own energy is a part of it, and the easier it will be for you to gain insights from its handling. While a card or letter might help you link yourself to them, a wedding or class ring, a favorite necklace, or other prized possession will work even better.

To use psychometry in an Automatic Writing, simply take the object in hand and allow yourself to spend a few minutes getting the "feel" of it. Hold it, think about it, focus on it, memorize it, try to sense the energy of the person emanating from its center, coming into you, and telling you what you need to know. Continue to hold this object in your non-writing hand as you begin the work.

Another way to connect with a person not present is through a chakra link. To use a chakra link you will need to plan the time of your Automatic Writing session with the person having the reading done. At the appointed time you will both begin connecting the energy of your chakra points, beginning with the Root Chakra. Visualize this as a vibrant beam of red, slow-moving light going out from yourself and meeting the Root Chakra of the person for whom you are reading.

Once the Root Chakra is connected, move to the next one and link it up. Continue working upwards in this way until all the chakras have been connected.

Visualize the connecting lights like this:

- Root Chakra—A dense, throbbing, slow-moving red beam.
- Navel Chakra—A bright orange shaft of light pulsating only slightly faster than the red.
- Solar Plexus—A radiant yellow, opaque light.
- Heart Center—A rich, verdant, leaf-green exuding love and harmony, moving at a medium speed.

- Throat Chakra—A pure, true blue beam of intense light.
- Third Eye—A quick-moving indigo beam which pulsates rapidly as it travels.
- Crown Chakra—A very fast-moving violet light that vibrates with an intensity that can be heard.

When you feel the connections have all has been made, you may begin your Automatic Writing as usual.

As time passes and you become more proficient in your art, you will find it becomes fairly easy to do Automatic Writing for others with little ritualized preparation. Just remember that for best results, the closer a bond you can form with your subject, the clearer and more precise your work will be.

Reading for Difficult People

No matter how mellow, loving, or "enlightened" we think we are, there will always be people who just "rub us the wrong way." Sometimes they are merely acquaintances, sometimes co-workers, and sometimes members of our own families.

So what do you do when asked to read for these people? How do you forge a working link with someone you are not particularly fond of? How do you connect with a difficult person?

Truthfully, chances are that you won't be able to do it. Your Higher Self will not allow you to waste your time and effort on things which it feels have no value for you. You may at best get random impressions that you can write down, but you will probably not be able to open up your psychic channels completely and allow the writing to flow.

So then, how do you handle the situation when this person knows how successfully you worked for another friend of yours? How do you avoid hurt feelings and embarrassment?

Your temporary impotence can be explained away diplomatically in one of two ways, both of which have firm roots in truth. First, you can tell this person that occasionally writings done for others do not always work because of some sort of emotional incompatibility. Secondly, you can explain that no matter how good you are at your craft you can experience off days. Both of these explanations are truthful and can be given with a clear conscience, without hurting feelings.

❦ 9 ❦

Interpreting Your Automatic Writing

Most of your Automatic Writing will come to you clearly, though you need to be aware that some of it will not. In order to accurately interpret the meaning of your communications you will need to understand the basics of language structure and the symbolic meaning of words.

We can categorize the Automatic Writing you will receive into one of four categories. Any and/or all might be present within any single communication: Plain Language; Metaphoric, Idiomatic, and Slang Language; Cryptic Language; and Symbolic or Archetypal Language.

Plain Language

Many people enjoy a good mystery, but too many people also like to create a mystery where one does not exist. In Automatic Writing it is often the uncluttered messages that confuse people because they are looking for the "mystery."

Plain language needs no explanation. This category of written communication is straightforward—all the words used mean exactly what they are supposed to mean, they are nearly dictionary-perfect in their usage, and there is nothing for you to struggle to interpret or hidden meanings for you to uncover. For example, if you find in your writing the sentence, "Your mother's illness is over and she is now healthy and out of danger," then that is probably exactly what it means and you shouldn't waste your time trying to read things into it that are simply not there.

Use your common sense. If an Automatic Writing seems open and honest, then give yourself a break and give it the benefit of the doubt.

Metaphoric, Idiomatic, and Slang Language

Metaphors are expressive phrases heard and read by millions every single day. They add to the descriptive quality of language. Unfortunately, they also can cause minor confusion when they appear in Automatic Writing.

A metaphor is defined as a figure of speech in which one object or action is likened to another in a way that makes the two seem indistinguishable. For example, "She is an angel in her service to others." We know when reading this sentence that the woman referred to is not actually an angel, but rather she takes on the perceived qualities of kindness, selflessness, and mercy when serving others. To assume this is saying that this woman is actually an angelic being is silly. Again, common sense is your guide to deciphering the exact meanings of your writing.

Idioms are found in all languages, especially those whose grammatical structures do not employ a formal case system such as English. They are the first cousins of slang, and they help to define and unite cultures and generations. An idiom is a phrase not readily understandable when its components are broken down, but which, as a whole, make perfect sense to those fluent in the particular language. The common American English phrases, "Just put up with it," and, "Get with it," are excellent examples of idioms. Those of us who speak English fluently readily grasp the meaning of both sentences, the first one meaning "to tolerate something" and the second meaning "to pay attention or to spring into action." But if we were to take apart the phrases word by word and analyze their individual meanings, we would find these sentences to be no more than a jumble of nonsense words. Think about it.... What do "put," a verb meaning "to place;" "up," meaning "to rise;" and "with," a preposition meaning "to accompany," have to do with the idea of tolerance?

These language types will be found in your Automatic Writing in greater or lesser quantities depending on what sort of entity you are contacting. Older beings will sometimes write to you in antiquated idioms that may require work to decode, and others may use modern slang. It will be left to you to spot these colorful phrases and interpret them accordingly.

Slang is a term for words that are faddish and popular. These words and phrases tend to come in and out of vogue every ten years or so. For example, in the early 1970s popular slang referred to something as "bad" if it were fashionable or fine. In the 1950s "bad" was "hip," and in the 1920s it was the "cat's pajamas." Again, only you can decide if the words on your written paper are slang, idioms, metaphors, or other colorful expressions that, though they don't make concrete sense, are easily interpretable.

Cryptic Language

Cryptic language is most often seen in response to questions about the future. It is closely related to symbolic language in that they both take a bit of detective work to determine their meanings. The difference is that, where symbols are meant to be decoded, cryptic messages often are not, or they are at the very least meant to make you work or wait to decipher them.

Often when we are asking questions in Automatic Writing whose answers might be unpleasant, hard to define, or obscure, we will receive responses that sound like they might have been part of the code of the French Underground during World War II, rather than replies to our current concerns and queries. But, despite this drawback, the answers we get in cryptic form are often the most intriguing and unforgettable ones we receive, and also the ones whose meanings often take a long time to come clear.

When I first began using Automatic Writing, I asked a question about someone who I thought might soon be playing a large role in my life, even though this was someone I had not yet met. The answer I received to my query is one I can quote from memory, "That one is fine and wants you to know."

Since the issue I asked about remains unresolved, I often think about this communication and wonder if this means that things are fine the way they are and I should forget about it, or that this person will still be coming to play a part in my life and I just have to keep waiting.

You will probably find, as I did, that Automatic Writing containing cryptic messages are the writings you turn back to again and again, looking for new insights each time you read them, sure that the solution lies in your hand, but unable to fully understand its meaning.

There is a good deal of controversy when-ever cryptic messages are received in any kind of divination. Those who would seek to debunk the entire process claim that the forthcoming answers are vague simply because they have to be either general enough to apply to any and all situations, or because there really are no answers. While in a small percentage of divinations this may be true, we have to look at two other options in order to make an educated assessment of our messages.

The future is changing for us each second as the human race writes and rewrites it, and any divination—including Automatic Writing—can only read and assess the potentials currently being set in motion by us. Sometimes events are changing so quickly that no single possible out-come emerges as the most likely answer. It is also reasonable to expect that in some cases there are answers we simply should not have or, deep down, do not really want to have. Our instinct for self-protection, with the aid of our Spirit Guides and our Higher Selves, simply will not allow us to know that which would be disturbing or detri-mental to us. Such knowledge certainly would keep us from functioning in the present by caus-ing the kind of fear and anticipation that would render us immobile.

Symbolic or Archetypal Language

Archetypes are the deeply symbolic prototypes that work the same on the minds of virtually all human beings regardless of their cultural background. The way they act or interact with other such symbols determines much of their meaning and ultimate effect.

If you find yourself sketching pictures on your writing pad, you will easily be able to see exactly what archetypal images have appeared. However, some psychologists argue that written words are not truly archetypes because they constitute a cognitive language and therefore are not truly symbolic. Others argue that language is nothing more than agreed-upon symbols for larger meanings. Written archetypes function the same way as picture symbols, especially if you are writing down a word from a random impression that comes to you as you practice Automatic Writing. Both can mean something other than what is readily apparent.

While most archetypes are the same for everyone, there will always be a few that have a special meaning for you, and only you can make these distinctions. For instance, if you have a morbid fear of snakes you should disregard the common symbol of rebirth they represent and interpret them from your own unique point-of-view. If you are told there is a "snake in your garden," this will probably not mean that a profound change or renewal is about to take place, but that your peace and security is about to be severely upset.

You may also come across entities who want to confuse your reverent sense of the occult by mentioning such mundane things as televisions or automobiles, items that are well on their way to becoming established archetypes as their presence batters the human psyche on a daily basis. Only you will be able to tell if your written words are actually references to these inherently modern items or if they are symbolic of a more profound message.

To get you started I have made an extensive list of some of the more common archetypal symbols, the ones you are most likely to come across in your Automatic Writing. As you study the chart you will understand what these are and how they are used. For more detailed information on archetypes, how they work, and how to interpret them for yourself, look into the writings of psychologist Carl Jung who spent his lifetime studying them. Or you might seek out the dream interpretation guides that are on the market. They often contain extensive lists of archetypes. Be sure to get the ones that discuss the symbols themselves and not the ones that attempt to use them as a means of predicting the future.

In order to begin to interpret the deeper meanings of these symbolic words, you will need to have the complete text of your Automatic Writing in front of you so that you can look at both the meanings of the individual words and at their meanings within the context of the rest of the writing. For example, if you have been asking a question about a strained friendship and you have in front of you the sentence, "The ring is broken," you should first look in the following list under "ring" and find: "Ring, broken." You will see that one of the probable meanings is 'infidelity." It is then possible to interpret this to mean that your friend has not been a faithful one. On the other hand, if your written text seems to be telling you that your friend still cares for you, "The beloved one only eludes your fist," you can see that a fist means "loss of freedom, greed," or "jealousy," and you may want to interpret this to mean that the relationship is only changing and that you should give your friend the freedom to grow and change if the relationship is to survive.

Begin now to study archetypes, both the written and the pictorial, and try to develop an intuitive feeling for what certain images and words mean. In doing this you will be much more successful, not only with your Automatic Writing, but in many other occult endeavors.

Symbol	Probable Meaning/Association
Abyss	Danger, clouded thinking, immobility
Acorn	Great potential
Altar	Holy, sacred, fear
Anchor	Something that holds you back
Apple, whole	Hidden desire
Apple, sliced	Fragmentation of self
Ashes	Protection, transformation, renewal
Ax, double	Duality, feminine principle, two sides to issue
Ax, single	Swiftness, judgment
Baby	Potential, innocence
Baby, crying	Distress, insecurity
Ball, bouncing	Lack of control
Ball, rolling	Lack of direction
Ball, stationary	Cycles
Barrel, empty	Poverty
Barrel, full	Prosperity
Barn, closed	Prosperity
Barn, open	Poverty
Basket	Completeness, union, sexuality, marriage
Bed	Lack of initiative, need to reconsider

Symbol	Probable Meaning/Association
Bee Hive	Abundance, or matters of the temple
Bees	Industry, team effort
Bells, ringing	Wish fulfillment, protection
Bells, still	Future unpredictable, defenses down/vulnerable
Belt	Confusion, restriction, self-control, high rank
Bird, dead	Dashed hopes
Bird, feeding	Preparation and planning
Bird, in flight	Success, the Higher Self
Bird, on ground	Potential for success
Black	The hidden, the womb, night, loss
Blood	Life, motherhood, power, energy, lust, rage
Blue	Spirituality
Book, closed	Untapped potential
Book, open	Knowledge, information
Bouquet	Fulfillment, honor/success
Bouquet, dry	Disappointment
Bow and arrow	Great potential
Bridge	Transition
Bridge/ water	Spiritual transition
Broom	New beginnings, completeness, the pure
Brown	Animals

Symbol	Probable Meaning/Association
Butterfly	Renewal, good health, news from afar
Cage	Restriction, imprisonment, suppression
Canopy	Home, family, marriage, union
Cat	Mystery, magick, fear, the night
Cauldron, empty	The womb, rebirth, goddess
Cauldron, full	Motherhood, abundance, fulfillment
Cave, entrance	Motherhood, journeys, secrets
Cave, interior	The womb
Cemetery	Loneliness, transition, that which is left
Chains	Suppressed emotions, fear, immobility
Chimney	Magick, travel, the soul, the spirit world
Chimney/ smoke	Happy home life, abundance
Cloak, alone	Hiding
Cloak, covering	Death, severe transformation, illness
Clouds, white	Spirituality, afterlife, peace
Clouds, dark	Storms, fear, unrest, impending danger
Comet	Mysteries revealed

Symbol	Probable Meaning/Association
Cross	Protection, the center
Crossroads	Protection, safety, the microcosm
Crow	Theft
Crown	Knowledge, rulership, intelligence
Crutch	Fear, immobility
Deer	Running from troubles
Deer, leaping	Overcoming obstacles
Desert	Barrenness, dashed hopes, long journey
Dog, alone	Loyalty, companionship, protection
Dog, howling	Warning
Dog, in pack	Strength, closed ranks
Door, closed	Energy blockage, secrets, frustration
Dove, ascend	Connection with Higher Self
Dove, descend	Peace, assurance, connected to deity
Dove, flying	Loss
Door, opened	Energy flow, defenses down, new worlds
Eagle	Personal power, the Higher Self
Eagle, flying	Success, Higher Self, safety
Ear	Omniscience, being on guard
Egg	Life

Symbol	Probable Meaning/Association
Egg, broken	Shattered hopes, poverty
Elderly people	Great wisdom
Eye	Deities, caution, omniscience
Faery, light	Otherworld matters, good fortune
Faery, dark	Materialism, bad luck
Fence	Obstacles, division, separation, immobility
Field, barren	Loss, destruction, hopes gone, infertility
Field, growing	Abundance, joy, fulfillment
Field, harvest	Success, rest
Fire	Energy, transformation
Fireplace, lit	Centrality, contentment at home, abundance
Fireplace, unlit	Loss of balance, loss of home, hatred
Fish, alone	Wealth
Fish, a pair	Confusion, unresolved issue, opposition
Fish, a school	Great wealth and abundance, knowledge
Fists	Greed, loss of freedom, jealousy
Flag	Sides taken, glory and honors, clannishness
Flower	Rebirth, spring, beginnings of success

Symbol	Probable Meaning/Association
Fog	The hidden, confusion, the materialistic
Gallows	Emergencies, fear of change
Garden	Personal concerns
Garden, bloom	Achievement, success, fertility
Garden, ruins	Stagnation, death, failure
Ghost	Unfulfilled potential, secrets revealed
Goat	Lust, abandon, occult wisdom
Gold	The sun, God, money, attainment
Grains	Fertility, abundance
Grapes	Hedonism, joy, successful harvest
Green	Fertility, potential, money, earth
Gun	Distrust, lies, war, fear, force, violence
Hammer	Labor
Hand, closed	Lies, argument
Hand, hidden	Greed, distrust
Hand, open	Friendship, protection
Harp	Spirituality, astral world matters, pleasure
Heart	Love, fidelity
Hen	Family matters, children, motherhood
Honey	Fulfillment of all desires

Symbol	Probable Meaning/Association
Horn	Harvest of abundance, union of opposites
Horse/feeding	Contentment, home life
Horse/off feet	Disaster, illness
Horse/running	Success, prosperity
House/familiar	Family, belonging, stability, shelter
House/strange	Longing, disconnectedness, suspicion
Horseshoe	Vast good fortune, protection
Horns	Power, rulership
Ice	Binding, rigidity, hatred, illness
Jail	To prevent from action, immobility, suppression
Jewelry	Wealth, vanity, honors
Key	Impediments, immobility due to fear, answers
Keyhole	Disclosure, a way without means, outsiders
Knife	Distrust
Knot	Immobility, difficulty, ideas not fruitful
Lace	Hiding under a false face, frivolity, vanity
Ladder	Way provided is difficult, threatened success
Lake	Hidden worlds

Symbol	Probable Meaning/Association
Lamp	The spirit, enlightenment, aid to seeker
Lantern	Enlightenment, hope, answers
Lark	Good fortune, achievement of goals
Lighthouse	Guidance
Lightning	Discord, sudden change, new ideas
Lion, lying	Indolence, those who wait
Lion, roaring	Kingship, strength
Lioness	Protection, ability to solve problems creatively
Lizard	Power of invisibility
Lock	Fear, bewilderment, exile
Mask	The hidden, the deities, ancestors
May Pole	Union/sex, marriage, festivities
Moon	Mystery, the goddess, womanhood
Mother	Security, unconditional love, fruition
Mountain	Personal challenge
Mountain range	Major obstacles
Necklace	Enslavement
Needles	Slander and gossip
Nest	Home, security, wealth
Oak	Strength and longevity

Symbol	Probable Meaning/Association
Oven	Fertility, success, abundance
Owl	Wisdom, night, mystery, illness
Palace	Wealth, rulership, or being shut out
Pie	Successful harvest
Pig	The divine feminine
Pink	Peace, romance
Pitchfork	Fertility, joy in labor, activity
Pyramid	Stability, ancient wisdom
Rainbow	Bridge between worlds, promises kept
Raven	An oracle
Red	Anger, lust, power, war
Rice	Sustenance, fertility, joy
Ring	Fidelity, belonging, completeness, unity
Ring, broken	Infidelity, change, divorce
Ring, insignia	Fraternity, leadership
River/dried	Loss, stagnation
River/flowing	Success and fulfillment, travel
River/frozen	Fear, immobility, lost potential
Road	Showing the way, movement
Road/fork	Decisions to be made, choices
Rooster	The sun, God, call to action
Scales	Matters of balance, justice, and retribution
Shawl	Acceptance, security

Symbol	Probable Meaning/Association
Sheep	Abundance of the material, or stupidity
Shepherd	Steadfastness, security, protection, love
Shield	Protection, security, guardedness, mother
Ship, aground	Danger, stagnation, disaste
Ship, in port	Dreams yet to be realized
Ship, sailing	Success, dream world, psychicism
Shovel	Labors coming to naught
Sickle	Change, harvest, death
Silver	The moon, the goddess, occult mystery
Sky	The macrocosm
Snake	Eternity, rebirth, change
Snow	Winter, death, purity, sleep
Spider	Creative potential, ability to overcome enemies
Spider Web	Intrigue, traps, creativity
Staff	Phallus, masculine power
Stairs	Pathways to the unknown
Sun	Newness, the God, summer, energy
Swan	Profound change
Sword	Phallus, war, protection
Table, empty	Destruction, loss, waiting
Table, full	Knowledge, success, leadership

Symbol	Probable Meaning/Association
Throne	Rulership, controversy
Tornado	Sweeping change
Tower	Inability to act, disaster
Trade	Peace, co-existence
Tree	The universe
Tree, fir	The goddess, eternity
Triangle	Stability, manifestation, the godhead
Trident	Manifestation, success, union, the sea
Tomb, closed	Life and life cycles, happiness
Tomb, open	Death and change, moving on
Tunnel	The birth canal
Turtle	Success, the unusual
Veil	Hidden with fear, deceit
Violet	The Higher Self, peace, psychic power
Viper	Treachery
Volcano	Violence, male power
Vulture	Disease, destruction, fear, violent change
Wand	Creativity, magick, the phallus
Water, calm	Birth, change, that which is hidden
Water, rough	Turmoil
Water Pump	Little gain for much effort
Waves	Inner-world matters, journeys, freedom

Symbol	Probable Meaning/Association
Weaver	A worker of magick, witch
Well	The birth canal, transition
Whale	Struggle
Wheel	Cycles, eternity, reincarnation
White	Purity, innocence, Higher Self, astral
Wind	A message, that which is in motion
Window/closed	Security, safety
Window/open	Loss, insecurity, vulnerability
Wine	Friendship, tight human bonds
Wolf	Fearlessness, loyalty
Wolves/pack	Family
Woods	The hidden, unseen potential, elementals
Worms	Energy sent in wrong direction, silly worries
Wreath	Eternity, the Wheel of the Year

Numbers as Archetypes

Numbers function as different archetypes within various cultures. For example, to the Celts and Norse people three was a sacred number, but to the Chinese it was unlucky.

The following list attempts to sort out some of this cultural mish-mash and provide you with a working guide to the deeper meanings of numbers.

0 — Beginnings and/or endings.

1 — The number of the Self in the west, but a symbol of loneliness and isolation in the east where living with supportive, extended families, and involvement in daily team work, are the norm.

2 — The number of union, polarity, or duality. Also a number of balance and potential. A lucky number in ancient Greece.

3 — The sacred number of the Celtic and Nordic people, but seen as unlucky in parts of the orient. Also a sacred number to the Hindus.

4 — The number of the elements. Seen almost universally as a number of balance and completeness. Also the principal sacred number of the Native Americans, and of the Shinto religion.

5 — Middle Eastern mysticism and medieval numerology teaches that this is a number of ill-luck.

6 — A number of balance to ancient Rome. A number of wholeness to the Native Americans.

7 — "Lucky Seven" is known almost universally, and is particularly strong in Christian mysticism.

8 — To the Chinese this is the most sacred number of all and represents life.

9 — A number of wholeness and sacredness to the Celts because it is three times three. Also the number usually associated with the moon.

10 — A number associated with the planet earth, and of the earth plane, in Kaballah.

13 — The traditional number of people in a coven or magick circle. Also the number of full moons in a solar year.

33 — Another sacred number to the Celts.

40 — Unlucky in Jewish mysticism.

50 — A number of completeness and abundance in Jewish mysticism. A number which signifies a time to help others and rejoice.

666 — The number of evil and destruction to many Christians.

777 — A sacred number in High Magick, one which often represents completion or manifestation of all things, and fulfillment.

888 — The number of perfection in Chinese numerology.

2000 — The approximate number of years in an astrological age.

❧ 10 ❧

Summing It All Up

Automatic Writing has many applications. It is an effective tool for divination, self-exploration, personal guidance, and spiritual growth. As you grow and mature with this oracle you will no doubt find new and creative ways it can help you.

Everyone experiences Automatic Writing a little differently. Don't give in to the temptation to compare your results to someone else's and then try to place an arbitrary value judgment on them. Repeat: If the messages you receive are of help and comfort to you then you are a success!

If you have finished your sixty-day efforts and are not succeeding as well as you would like, take a break, and come back to another sixty-day session in a few weeks. During that time allow yourself to think about the forces preventing your success. Often you may simply be having difficulties because of temporary job stress. Don't get discouraged!

Ultimately, only you can decide how much time and effort you feel is worth putting into your Automatic Writing. For those who persevere and succeed, the rewards are great.

❧ Glossary ❧

Akashic Records—A term used synonymously with **Collective Unconscious**, the place where all the information about anything and anyone that ever was, is, or will be is stored. Occultists and other New Age thinkers believe that the information contained here can be accessed through controlled altered states of consciousness. Famed psychic Edgar Cayce believed these records were the source of his accurate psychic readings. The word Akashic comes from the Hindustani word *akasha* which means "spirit."

Altered state of consciousness—See **Meditation**.

Amulet—A natural object reputed to give protection to the carrier. Amulets are items such as stones or fossils and are not to be confused with man-made talismans.

Archetype—Archetypes are universal symbols defined by Funk and Wagnalls as a "standard pattern" or a "prototype." They speak to our subconscious minds; are the potent images that cloud our dreams; and the machinery that makes all forms of divination possible.

Aromatherapy—The inhaling of concentrated scents to produce changes in the body and/or mind, or as a medium to working magick.

Astral projection—The art of "leaving one's body" or "lucid dreaming" whereby someone in a trance state visits other locations, realms, or times. This is often referred to as traveling on the **Astral Plane**, generally conceptualized as an invisible parallel world unseen in our own world of form.

Astrology—The study of and belief in the effects the movements and placements of planets and other heavenly bodies have on the lives and behavior of human beings.

Aura—The energy field surrounding all living things. The aura can be seen easily by psychics, and also by others who train themselves to see it. Some people like to infuse their auras with gold, silver, or white light to surround themselves with protection during psychic experimentation.

Automatic Writing—The art of contacting other intelligences through the use of a pencil and paper while in an altered state of consciousness.

Auto-suggestion—A form of self-hypnosis where a positive, present-tense affirmation is repeated to one's self over and over while in a receptive, altered state of consciousness. The idea of this exercise is to convince the mind that an alternative reality is, in fact, concrete reality, thereby enlisting its help to manifest the desired change.

Binding ritual—A ritualized magickal ceremony in which some object is bound to a single person. In the case of Automatic Writing, a binding ritual often involves a specific ritual designed by the writer to bind the writing hand to its owner so that no unwelcome movement can occur.

Ceremonial magick—A highly codified magickal tradition based on Kaballah, the Jewish and Christian Gnostic mystical teachings.

Chakra—This term comes from Hindustani and is used to define the energy centers of the human body. The seven principal chakra centers are located at the base of the tail bone, at the navel, the solar plexus, the heart center, the breast bone, the throat, the Third Eye, and just above the crown of the head. These centers can be energized to promote good health, spirit contact, psychicism, and a host of other physical and spiritual benefits.

Channeling—Allowing one's self to be used as a vessel for a discarnate being or spirit to speak through.

Charging—The act of empowering an herb, stone, or other magickal object with one's own energies through willpower and visualization. These are then directed outwards toward a specific goal. For example, herbs or other objects can be charged with energy to aid with protection or spirit contact during Automatic Writing. Charging is synonymous with **Enchanting, Empowering or Programming**.

Circle—The protective sacred space wherein all magick is to be worked and all ritual contained. The circle contains raised energy and provides protection, and is created and banished with one's own energy.

Clearing ritual—A protective ritual designed to clear away negative or unwanted vibrations from a designated area.

Collective unconscious—A term used to describe the sentient connection of all living things, past and present. It is synonymous with the terms "deep mind" and "Higher Self." This is believed to be the all-knowing energy source that contains the entire sum of human knowledge and experience tapped during divination. Also see **Akashic Records**.

Conscious mind—That part of the brain we have access to in the course of a normal, waking day. It is the part of the mind that holds retrievable memory and other easy to recall information.

Corpus callosum—The connecting tissues that join the right and left hemispheres of the brain.

Crown chakra—The chakra located just above the head which is visualized as a rapidly pulsating violet sphere.

Deep mind—An occult term used synonymously with sub- and/or super-conscious mind. It is a conceptualization rather than an actual place, and is considered to be that part of us which can communicate with the Higher Self and which we use when doing an altered state of consciousness exercise.

Deity—An inclusive term for a Goddess or God.

Deosil—The act of moving, working, or dancing in a clockwise motion. This is the traditional direction one works with for creative magick. Deosil is also called **Sunwise**.

Divination—The act of divining the future by reading potentials currently in motion. Divination can be done through meditation, scrying, astral projection, with cards, stones, or any number of means. The most popular forms of divination today are **Tarot, Runes, Pendulums, Scrying**, and the controversial **Ouija™ board**.

Discarnate—A non-corporeal being who may or may not have once been a living human being, or a being inhabiting another plane of existence that co-exists with the earth plane known to humans. Also see **Ghost**.

Earth plane—A metaphor for your normal waking consciousness.

Element—The four alchemical elements once thought to make up the entire universe. They are Earth, Air, Fire and Water plus the fifth element of pure spirit in, of, and outside them all.

Ephemeris—An astrological/astronomical calendar that shows exactly where in the heavens each planet and asteroid is located at any given time in relation to earth.

Ghost—The intact, sentient spirit or soul of a deceased human, often referred to in New Age/Pagan terms as a "human discarnate." Many believe these spirits can be contacted by various means such as through seances or deep meditations.

Grimoire—A practical book of magickal spells and rituals.

Grounding—To disperse excess energy generated during any magickal or occult rite by sending it into the earth. It can also mean the process of centering one's self in the physical world both before and after any ritual or astral experience.

Heart center—The chakra located at the center of the breast bone which is visualized as a sphere of green.

Herbalism—The art of using herbs to facilitate human needs both magickally and medically.

Higher Self—That part of us that connects our corporeal minds to the Collective Unconscious and with the divine knowledge of the universe. It is often visualized as being connected to the crown chakra.

Incense, ritual—The ritualized burning of herbs, oils, or other aromatic items to scent the air during acts of magick, ritual, divination, etc., to help one better attune with the energies of their goal.

Kaballistic—Related to the KABALLAH, the body of Jewish-Gnostic mystical works.

Karma—A Hindustani word which reflects the ancient belief that good and evil done will return to be visited on a person either in this life or in a succeeding one.

Latin cross—The universal symbol of Christianity. This symbol can be used as one of protection during divinations and other psychic work.

Lotus position—The meditation posture from the Eastern occult school which has the legs crossed, and the outer sides of the feet drawn up over the top of the knees. A half-Lotus position uses only one foot over one knee.

Magick—Spelled with a 'k' to differentiate it from the magic of stage illusions. The best definition of magick was probably invented by infamous ceremonial magician Aleister Crowley: "Magick is the science and art of causing change to occur in conformity to will."

Meditation—A deliberate attempt to slow the cycles per second of one's brain waves to generate a consciously controlled sleeping state. One is said to be in meditation, or in an altered state of consciousness, when the brain waves are deliberately taken to any level below what is called Beta, or normal waking consciousness. Also called **Meditative State, Altered State, Going Down, and Trance State**.

Medium—A term used to describe a person who is being used as a physical channel through which a discarnate spirit communicates. If you contact discarnates during Automatic Writing you are practicing mediumship.

Metaphysics—A philosophy that seeks to explore the theoretical realm of the hard sciences. Metaphysics also seeks to resolve the abstract concepts of reality versus imagination, and the origin, nature, and foundation of religious beliefs and practices.

Mudra position—A meditative posture for the hands from the Eastern and Aryan occult schools that has the hands resting on the upper legs with the palms facing upward. The thumb and forefinger of each hand are gently pressed together.

Navel—The chakra located just below the navel which is visualized as a sphere of orange.

New Age—While this term is usually used to denote persons interested in applying metaphysics to everyday living experiences, it is made up of teachings that are very old. These include self-determination, expanded consciousness and awareness, belief in reincarnation, and self-healing. Many people believe the beginning of the New Age coincides with the astrological age of Aquarius whose exact boundaries are unknown, but is believed to begin sometime between the years 1900 and 2100.

Occult—Literally means "hidden" and is broadly applied to a wide range of metaphysical topics which lie outside of the accepted realm of mainstream theologies. Such topics include, but are not limited to, divination, hauntings, spirit communication, natural magick, ceremonial magick, alternative spirituality, psychic phenomena, alchemy, astrology, demonology, the study of the spiritual practices of ancient civilizations, and the study of any of these topics as applied to mainstream religions.

Occultist—One who practices and/or studies a variety of occult subjects.

Oracle—A method of obtaining prophecies or a method of divination. Also used outside of New Age circles to refer to any infallible source.

Pagan—Generic term for anyone who practices an earth or nature religion. The word is sometimes used synonymously with "Witchcraft."

Paranormal—A word coined to describe events which are not considered "normal" under the known laws of physical science, but which, nonetheless, continue to occur. It is believed by many that laws that govern these events do exist, but they are simply not known to us at this time.

Parapsychology—A sister science of psychology (some say a pseudo-science) which studies psychic phenomenon, particularly as it pertains to spirit contact and manifestation. Automatic Writing is one of the many areas of interest to parapsychologists.

Past-life regression—The act of using meditation or guided meditation to pass through the veil of linear time and perceive experiences encountered in a previous existence.

Pentagram—The five-pointed star which has come to symbolize Western Paganism. It is an ancient symbol with multiple meanings, and can be used as a symbol of protection during divinations and other psychic work.

Planetary hours—A system of astrology that divides each twenty-four hour day into individual blocks of time governed by the influence of the seven major planets. The earliest known use of this system dates to the fourteenth century.

Poppets—Anthropomorphic dolls used to represent certain human beings in magickal spells. These have been associated with the negative aspects of Voodoo, but they also serve positive purposes such as in healing rituals and binding spells.

Possession—A state in which a person is, or appears to be, under the control of another being inhabiting his or her physical body. Most cases are either the result of fear projections or mental imbalances.

Prana—An ancient Indian word meaning "controlled breathing." Prana was central to Aryan beliefs about connecting the earth-bound mind to other forms of consciousness. They discovered that by varying the length and depth of the breath one could attain various levels of conscious and super-conscious awareness. This idea has been adapted into nearly every modern occult school of thought.

Precognition—The psychic phenomenon of knowing about something before it happens. Precognitive messages are frequently a part of Automatic Writing.

Protection ritual—A systematic set of words and/or gestures which the worker of the ritual believes will render him or her impervious to harm.

Psychic research—The study of psychic phenomenon, particularly as it relates to human contact with discarnate human spirits. Also called "Psychical Research."

Psychometry—The art of gleaning information about a person, or connecting with their energy, by holding in one's hand an object that has been held, worn, or owned by that person.

Reading—A general term for performing divination. Even though you are writing rather than reading (as in Runes or Cards), Automatic Writing is still referred to as giving or doing a reading.

Reincarnation—The belief that the souls of living things return to the earth plane in another body after death. Concepts about how this works vary with religious traditions and individuals. The most sensitive area of conflict is in the controversy between those people who believe in a single omnipresent now in which all our lives are lived at once, and those who believe our lives are lived in a linear succession.

Retrocognition—The psychic phenomenon of possessing information from a time beyond the normal range of knowledge such as from one's own infancy or from a time before one's own birth.

Ritual—A systematic, formal or informal, prescribed set of rites whose purpose is to imprint a lasting change on the life and psyche of the participant.

Ritual tools—A general name for magickal or ritual tools used by a witch, magician, or practitioner of any religious or ceremonial working. These tools and their use varies by tradition.

Root chakra—The chakra located at the base of the tail bone. It is visualized as a slowly throbbing red sphere.

Rose cross—Also called an Equilateral Cross. This upright, equal-armed cross is an ancient symbol of balance and protection and can be used as such during divinations or other psychic work.

Runes—The ancient writing of the Teutonic people which is considered a magickal alphabet and has been adapted to divination.

Sacred writings—Also called Holy Writings. These are the sacred books of wisdom, legends, and learning declared holy, and sometimes infallible, by various religions. The sacred writings of one school of theology are not necessarily sacred to another.

Scrying—The divinatory act of gazing at an object or candle until prophetic visions appear.

Sigil—A symbol designed as a representation of a specific energy that contains within itself the power essence of that which it depicts.

Solar plexus—The location of the third chakra. It is visualized as a sphere of yellow.

Spirit guides—Discarnate beings who are entrusted with aiding a living person through life. Many people claim to have met their Spirit Guides and to consult them on a regular basis through Automatic Writing, Meditation, Dream Work, etc.

Star of David—This interlaced, six-pointed star has become the symbol of the Jewish religion. It is also one of the oldest symbols of creation and protection known to humankind. It can be an effective protective device during divination or other psychic work.

Subconscious mind—That part of the mind which functions below the levels we are able to access in the course of a normal, waking day. This area stores symbolic knowledge, dreams, and the tiniest details of every experience ever had by a person. This is sometimes referred to in New Age writings as the **Super-Conscious Mind**.

Supernatural—Another term for the **Paranormal**.

Talisman—An object believed to offer protection or other magickal service to the carrier. It differs from an amulet by being constructed and charged by the person using it rather than being an item found in nature.

Tarot—A set of cards containing potent symbols that can be read by the subconscious in order to do divination. The origin of the cards is unknown, but some guess that they originated in the Middle East around 3,000 years ago.

Telepathy—Receiving information from the mind of another person via the thought process alone. The energy of telepathy helps enable one person to perform divinations, such as Automatic Writing, for another.

Threefold Law—The karmic principle of Paganism. It states that any energy released by the witch or magician, either positive or negative, will return to the sender three times over.

Third Eye—The chakra located between and just above the eyes which is visualized as a sphere of indigo. This sphere is often associated with psychicism.

Thought form—An idea so often and intently conceived of, mulled over, and projected that it becomes real on other planes of existence and in the Collective Unconscious. Thought forms take on their greatest solidity when realized by groups of people rather than by individuals.

Throat chakra—The chakra located in the hollow of the throat which is visualized as a rich true blue.

Trance state—See **Meditation**.

Widdershins—This Germanic word means to go backwards, and in New Age/Pagan terms, it is the act of moving, working, walking, or dancing counter-clockwise in order to banish, diminish, close, or finish something, or to counter a negative force.

Xeno-escrite—The rare phenomenon of writing in a language unknown to the writer. The term comes from the Greek *xeno*, meaning "strange or foreign," and the French *escritre*, meaning "to write."

Xenoglossy—The rare phenomenon of speaking in a language unknown to the speaker. The term comes from the Greek *xeno*, meaning "strange or foreign," and the Latin *glossa*, meaning "speech" or "the tongue."

Zodiac—A theoretical belt of space encircling the earth that is divided into twelve "signs of the zodiac," each bearing the name of its corresponding constellation.

Zodiac wand—A magickal tool for transmitting etheric energy which uses the signs of the zodiac as a catalyst.

❧ Suggested Readings ❧

There are many books on the market covering New Age topics, stone lore, herbalism, channeling, divination, etc. I encourage you to read all you can about the occult subjects that interest you. Keep an open mind and read critically. Immediately put aside any book whose author states that his or her way is the only right one, or who attempts to coerce you into doing anything you feel is wrong.

The following books, listed by subject, are ones I have found to be well-written and insightful, and which I believe are writen by people whose personal ethics and teachings maintain the highest standards of integrity.

- The chakra system:

    Judith, Anodea. *Wheels of Life*. St. Paul, MN: Llewellyn Publications, 1986.

- Self-exploration:

    Sutphen, Dick. *Finding Your Answers Within*. New York: Pocket Books, 1989.

- Protection, divination:

     Gonzalez-Wippler, Migene. *The Complete Book of Spells, Ceremonies and Magic*. St. Paul, MN: Llewellyn Publications, 1988.

- Occult/magickal uses of color:

     Buckland, Raymond. *Practical Color Magic*. St. Paul, MN: Llewellyn Publications, 1987.

     Amber, Reuben. *Color Therapy*. Santa Fe, NM: Aurora Press, 1983.

- Herbal teas, oils, incenses, etc.:

     Cunningham, Scott. *The Complete Book of Incense, Oils and Brews*. St. Paul, MN: Llewellyn Publications, 1989.

     Cunningham, Scott. *Cunningham's Encyclopedia of Magical Herbs*. St. Paul, MN: Llewellyn Publications, 1986.

- Occult uses of aromatherapy:

     Cunningham, Scott. *Magical Aromatherapy*. St. Paul, MN: Llewellyn Publications, 1989.

- Astrological/planetary influences:

     The Daily Planetary Guide. St. Paul, MN: Llewellyn Publications. (These annuals are published each autumn for the following year, as they have been for most of this century. They contain information on all astrological phenomena along with an ephemeris for each month.)

- Art of visualization:

  > Denning, Melita, and Osborne Phillips. *Creative Visualization*. St. Paul, MN: Llewellyn Publications, 1987.

- Psychic protection:

  > Denning, Melita, and Osborne Phillips. *Psychic Self-Defense and Well-Being*. St. Paul, MN: Llewellyn Publications, 1986.

- Past-lives:

  > McClain, Florence Wagner. *The Llewellyn Practical Guide to Past-Life Regression*. St. Paul, MN: Llewellyn Publications, 1987.

  > Andrews, Ted. *How to Uncover Your Past Lives*. St. Paul, MN: Llewellyn Publications, 1992.

- Archetypes and the human psyche:

  > Jung, Carl G. *Man and His Symbols*. New York: Doubleday, 1964.

  > Lewis, Ralph M. *Behold the Sign: Ancient Symbolism*. San Jose, CA: Publishing Department of the Supreme Grand Lodge of AMORC (12th edition, 2nd printing), 1987 (originally published in 1944).

- Metaphysical uses of stones:

  > Cunningham, Scott. *Crystal, Gem and Metal Magic*. St. Paul, MN: Llewellyn Publications, 1988.

  > Mella, Dorothee L. *Stone Power*. New York: Warner Books, 1988.

- How the human brain works:

      Russell, Peter. *The Brain Book*. New York: Hawthorn Books, Inc., 1979.

      Rosenfeld, Albert, ed. *Mind and Supermind*. New York: Holt, Rinehart and Winston, 1977.

- Psychical research:

      Wilson, Colin. *Beyond the Occult: A Twenty Year Investigation Into the Paranormal*. New York: Carroll and Graf Publishers, Inc., 1988.

- Spirit contact:

      Merrill, Joseph. *Mediumship*. Indianapolis, IN: Summit Publications, 1981.

- Personality survival after physical death:

      Steiger, Brad and Sherry Hansen Steiger. *Undying Love*. New York: Berkley Books, 1992.

- Controlled breathing:

      Zi, Nancy. *The Art of Breathing*. New York: Bantam Books, 1986.

- Basic metaphysics:

      Fischella, Anthony J. *Metaphysics: The Science of Life*. St. Paul, MN: Llewellyn Publications, 1984.

❧ Addresses ❧

Capriland's Herb Farm
Silver Street
Coventry, CT O6238
(Write for free list of dried herbs and herbal books. Capriland also has special classes on herb use and hosts herbal lunches at various times throughout the year. Reservations are a must!)

Circle
P.O. Box 219
Mt. Horeb, WI 53572
(Circle sells printed and recorded music written by and for followers of the various earth religions. Some of the music is suitable for meditation, divination, etc. Request a sample copy of their excellent periodical for more information. Sample copy $4.50.)

Companion Plants
7247 N. Coolville Ridge Rd.
Athens, OH 457O1
(Sells herbs, oils, and live plants. Catalog $2.00.)

Craft of the Wise
45 Grove Street
New York, NY 10014
(Sellers of herbs, oils, books, tapes, magickal tools, and other occult paraphernalia. Request free catalog.)

Herbal Endeavors
3618 S. Emmons Ave.
Rochester Hills, MI 48063
(Sells herbs and essential oils. Catalog $2.50.)

Indiana Botanical Gardens
P.O. Box 5
Hammond, IN 46325
(Sellers of herbs, teas, charcoal blocks, herbal medicines and some books on alternative health care. Request free catalog.)

Isis Metaphysical
5701 E. Colfax
Denver, CO 80220
(Write for information as catalog price varies. Isis carries books, jewelry, incense, oils, herbs and periodicals. It is also a pleasant gathering center for Pagans, magicians, and other New Age thinkers. Be sure and obtain a list of their upcoming workshops, lectures, and classes.)

Lapidary Journal
P.O. Box 80937
San Diego, CA 92138
(This is a publication for rock collectors which contains information on stone origins and their lore. It also has ads from companies which sell stones, tumblers, jewelry mountings, etc. Write for subscription information.)

Leydet Oils
P.O. Box 2354
Fair Oaks, CA 95628
(Sellers of fine essential oils. Catalog and price list is currently $2.00)

Llewellyn's New Worlds of Mind and Spirit
P.O. Box 64383
Dept. 269
St. Paul, MN 55164-0383
(Sellers and publishers of books on metaphysics, magick, paganism, astrology, divination, women's studies, channneling, New Age interests, and alternative spirituality. Also deals in self-help products, Tarot cards, and other divinatory devices. One year's subscription $10.00)

The Magic Door
P.O. Box 8349
Salem, MA 01971
(Magickal and ritual supplies including books
and tarot cards. Request free catalog and ordering
information.)

Moon Scents and Magickal Blends, Inc.
P.O. Box 1588-C
Cambridge, MA 02238
(Sells all manner of magickal paraphernalia and
books and specializes in ritual oils and herbs.
Request free catalog.)

Mountain Butterfly Herbs
106 Roosevelt Lane
Hamilton, MT 59840
(Write for current information and prices with a
self-addressed stamped envelope.)

Sacred Spirit Products
P.O. Box 8163
Salem, MA 01971-8163
(Sellers of books, magickal tools, herbs, incense,
and other occult items. Catalog $3.00)

Sandy Mush Herb Nursery
Rt. 2, Surrett Cove
Lancaster, NC 28748
(Has over 800 in-stock herbs, dye plants, and other foliage. catalog contains interesting herbal tips as well as recipes.Catalog $4.00, refundable with your first order.)

Winners!
Valley of the Sun Publishing
P.O. Box 683
Ashland, OR 97520-0023
(Publishers and sellers of New Age music designed for use during meditation. They also produce excellent mind-body videos and audio tapes, including tapes to aid meditation, past-life recall, astral projection, healing, and many other areas of interest to New Age thinkers. First copy of their mag-a-log is free upon request, and will continue be sent free for up to a year if you order from them.)

STAY IN TOUCH

On the following pages you will find some of the books now available on related subjects. Your book dealer stocks most of these and will stock new titles in the Llewellyn series as they become available. We urge your patronage.

To obtain our full catalog write for our bimonthly news magazine/catalog, *Llewellyn's New Worlds of Mind and Spirit*. A sample copy is free, and it will continue coming to you at no cost as long as you are an active mail customer. Or you may subscribe for just $10.00 in the U.S.A. and Canada ($20.00 overseas, first class mail). Many bookstores also have *New Worlds* available to their customers. Ask for it.

Llewellyn's New Worlds of Mind and Spirit
P.O. Box 64383-K662-9, St. Paul, MN 55164-0383, U.S.A.

TO ORDER BOOKS AND TAPES

If your book dealer does not have the books described, you may order them directly from the publisher by sending full price in U.S. funds, plus $3.00 for postage and handling for orders *under* $10.00; $4.00 for orders *over* $10.00. There are no postage and handling charges for orders over $50.00. Postage and handling rates are subject to change. We ship UPS whenever possible. Delivery guaranteed. Provide your street address as UPS does not deliver to P.O. Boxes. UPS to Canada requires a $50.00 minimum order. Allow 4-6 weeks for delivery. Orders outside the U.S.A. and Canada: Airmail—add retail price of book; add $5.00 for each non-book item (tapes, etc.); add $1.00 per item for surface mail. Mail orders to:

LLEWELLYN PUBLICATIONS
P.O. Box 64383-K662-9, St. Paul, MN 55164-0383, U.S.A.

HOW TO DEVELOP & USE PSYCHOMETRY
by Ted Andrews

What if a chair could speak? What if you could pick up a pen and tell what kind of day its owner had had? What if you could touch someone and know what kind of person he or she truly was—or sense pain or illness? These examples just scratch the surface of the applications of psychometry: the ability to read the psychic imprints that exist upon objects, people and places.

Everyone is psychic. Unfortunately, most of the time we brush aside our psychic impressions. Now, everyone can learn to develop their own natural sensitivities. *How to Develop and Use Psychometry* will teach you to assess your own abilities and provide you with a step-by-step process for developing your natural psychic abilities, including over 25 exercises to heighten your normal sense of touch to new levels of sensitivity.

With a little awareness and practice, you can learn to use your inborn intuitive abilities to read the history of objects and places … locate missing or lost articles … develop intimacy… even find missing persons. *How to Develop and Use Psychometry* gives you all of the techniques you need to effectively "touch" the natural psychic within yourself!
1-56718-025-6, mass market, 224 pp., illus.

$3.99

HOW TO DREAM YOUR LUCKY LOTTO NUMBERS
by Raoul Maltagliati

Until now, there has been no scientific way to predict lotto numbers : they come up by chance. But tonight, you may find them through a trip into the dimension of the collective unconscious, where "time" and "chance" as we know them do not exist. Discover how to use this time-honored system of prediction that has been passed down through generations in Italy.

This book has been newly reprinted with an expanded Dream Dictionary and a new section "Meeting with a Dream Interpreter." You will meet an actual dream interpreter, who uses his skills to guide people in picking their lotto numbers. You will learn why you dream, how to isolate a dream's key points for clues to your lotto numbers, how to find the numeric equivalents of dream subjects, how to adjust for the Moon's influence on your dreams, and the importance of the day and month of your dreams.

0-87542-483-X, 208 pgs., mass market, illus.

$3.95

HOW TO HEAL WITH COLOR
by Ted Andrews
Now, for perhaps the first time, color therapy is placed within the grasp of the average individual. Anyone can learn to facilitate and accelerate the healing process on all levels with the simple color therapies in *How to Heal with Color*.

Color serves as a vibrational remedy that interacts with the human energy system to stabilize physical, emotional, mental and spiritual conditions. When there is balance, we can more effectively rid ourselves of toxins, negativities and patterns that hinder our life processes.

This book provides color application guidelines that are beneficial for over 50 physical conditions and a wide variety of emotional and mental conditions. Receive simple and tangible instructions for performing "muscle testing" on yourself and others to find the most beneficial colors. Learn how to apply color therapy through touch, projection, breathing, cloth, water and candles. Learn how to use the little known but powerful color-healing system of the mystical Qabala to balance and open the psychic centers. Plus, discover simple techniques for performing long distance healings on others.

0-87542-005-2, 240 pgs., mass market, illus.

$3.95

HOW TO MAKE AND USE A MAGIC MIRROR
Psychic Windows into New Worlds
by Donald Tyson
Tyson takes you step-by-step through the creation of this powerful mystical tool. You will learn about: tools and supplies needed to create the mirror; construction techniques; how to use the mirror for scrying (divination); how to communicate with spirits; and how to use the mirror for astral travel.

Tyson also presents a history of mirror lore in magic and literature. For anyone wanting their personal magical tool, *How to Make and Use a Magic Mirror* is a must item.
0-87542-831-2, 176 pgs., mass market, illus.

$3.95

HOW TO MEET & WORK WITH SPIRIT GUIDES
by Ted Andrews

We often experience spirit contact in our lives but fail to recognize it for what it is. Now you can learn to access and attune to beings such as guardian angels, nature spirits and elementals, spirit totems, archangels, gods and goddesses—as well as family and friends after their physical death.

Contact with higher soul energies strengthens the will and enlightens the mind. Through a series of simple exercises, you can safely and gradually increase your awareness of spirits and your ability to identify them. You will learn to develop an intentional and directed contact with any number of spirit beings. Discover meditations to open up your subconscious. Learn which acupressure points effectively stimulate your intuitive faculties. Find out how to form a group for spirit work, use crystal balls, perform automatic writing, attune your aura for spirit contact, use sigils to contact the great archangels and much more! Read *How to Meet and Work with Spirit Guides* and take your first steps through the corridors of life beyond the physical.
0–87542–008–7, 192 pgs., mass market, illus.

$3.95

HOW TO READ THE TAROT
The Keyword System
by Sylvia Abraham

In as little as one week's time you could be amazing your friends with the accuracy of your insights, when you study the easy-to-learn Keyword system of Tarot reading! Here is a simple and practical guide to interpreting the symbolic language of the Tarot that anyone can quickly learn to use with any Tarot deck.

Unlike other Tarot books that provide key word interpretations, *How to Read the Tarot* provides an interpretive structure that applies to the card numbers of both the Major *and* Minor Arcana. In the Keyword system, for example, every number "Two" card (the Two card of each suit in the Minor Arcana as well as the High Priestess, the Two card of the Major Arcana) has a basic "I KNOW" key phrase. These simple key phrases are then combined with the symbolic meaning of the four suits, to give you a rich source from which to draw your interpretations. The book includes five spreads and a dictionary of symbols.

Few Tarot books on the market are as concise and accessible as this one—and no other book shows how to use this unique system.

1-56718-001-9, 272 pgs., mass market, softcover

$4.99

HOW TO SEE AND READ THE AURA
by Ted Andrews
Everyone has an aura—the three-dimensional, shape-and-color-changing energy field that surrounds all matter. And anyone can learn to see and experience the aura more effectively. There is nothing magical about the process. It simply involves a little understanding, time, practice and perseverance.

Do some people make you feel drained? Do you find some rooms more comfortable and enjoyable to be in? Have you ever been able to sense the presence of other people before you actually heard or saw them? If so, you have experienced another person's aura. In this practical, easy-to-read manual, you receive a variety of exercises to practice alone and with partners to build your skills in aura reading and interpretation. Also, you will learn to balance your aura each day to keep it vibrant and strong so others cannot drain your vital force.

Learning to see the aura not only breaks down old barriers—it also increases sensitivity. As we develop the ability to see and feel the more subtle aspects of life, our intuition unfolds and increases, and the childlike joy and wonder of life returns.
0-87542-013-3, 160 pgs., mass market, illus.

$3.95

HOW TO UNCOVER YOUR PAST LIVES
by Ted Andrews

Knowledge of your past lives can be extremely rewarding. It can assist you in opening to new depths within your own psychological makeup. It can provide greater insight into present circumstances with loved ones, career and health. It is also a lot of fun.

Now Ted Andrews shares with you nine different techniques that you can use to access your past lives. Between techniques, Andrews discusses issues such as karma and how it is expressed in your present life; the source of past life information; soul mates and twin souls; proving past lives; the mysteries of birth and death; animals and reincarnation; abortion and pre-mature death; and the role of reincarnation in Christianity.

To explore your past lives, you need only use one or more of the techniques offered. Complete instructions are provided for a safe and easy regression. Learn to dowse to pinpoint the years and places of your lives with great accuracy, make your own self-hypnosis tape, attune to the incoming child during pregnancy, use the tarot and the cabala in past life meditations, keep a past life journal and more.

0-87542-022-2, 240 pgs., mass market, illus.

$3.95

THE LLEWELLYN PRACTICAL GUIDE TO THE DEVELOPMENT OF PSYCHIC POWERS
by Denning & Phillips
You may not realize it, but you already have the ability to use ESP, Astral Vision and Clairvoyance, Divination, Dowsing, Prophecy, and Communication with Spirits.

Written by two of the most knowledgeable experts in the world of psychic development, this book is a complete course—teaching you, step-by-step, how to develop these powers that actually have been yours since birth. Using the techniques, you will soon be able to move objects at a distance, see into the future, know the thoughts and feelings of another person, find lost objects and locate water using your no-longer latent talents.

Psychic powers are as much a natural ability as any other talent. You'll learn to play with these new skills, working with groups of friends to accomplish things you never would have believed possible before reading this book. The text shows you how to make the equipment you can use, the exercises you can do—many of them at any time, anywhere—and how to use your abilities to change your life and the lives of those close to you. Many of the exercises are presented in forms that can be adapted as games for pleasure and fun, as well as development.
0-87542-191-1, 272 pgs., 5 1/4 x 8, illus., softcover
$8.95